MONEY AND WEALTH

A Lifetime of Learning, Book 2

Mark Andre Alexander

Make clear distinctions,
and examine all things well.
*The Golden Verses of
Pythagoras*

THE SCHOOL OF
PYTHAGORAS™

Auburn, CA

Published by Mark Andre Alexander
P.O. Box 5286, Auburn, CA 95604-5286

First Edition

Library of Congress Cataloging-in-Publication Data

Alexander, Mark Andre, 1956-
Money and wealth: a lifetime of learning / by Mark Andre
Alexander

p. cm. — (A Lifetime of Learning, Book 2)
ISBN 978-1-937597-21-4

Cover design by Melinda De Ross: www.coveredbymelinda.com

Photos and illustrations are created by the author, in the public
domain, or licensed from Photos.com˝, PhotoDisc˚,
Thinkstock.com, and Nova Development Corporation.

Version 2_2

Formatted for iPad and other tablets.

Thanks to my readers: Bree, Scott, Frank, and Christine. Also,
thanks to BubbleCow.Com for their great book editing services
at a reasonable price.

Go to MarkAndreAlexander.Com to access a free 36-day course
on *Creating Your Life*.

Subscribe to the "Creating Your Life" channel on YouTube.

Books by Mark Andre Alexander

Creating Your Life (A Lifetime of Learning, Book 1)
Money and Wealth (A Lifetime of Learning, Book 2)
Sex and Romance (A Lifetime of Learning, Book 3)
Mozart and Great Music (A Lifetime of Learning, Book 4)

Handbook for Advanced Souls: Eternal Reminders for the Present Moment

Public domain works edited by Mark Andre Alexander

Hamlet and the Scottish Succession by Lilian Winstanley
Shakespeare's Law and Latin by Sir George Greenwood, M.P.
The George Greenwood Collection

CONTENTS

For Bree and HK,
and those who Quest

About This Series

How many times have we said it to ourselves?

If I only knew then what I know now?

This series of little books, titled *A Lifetime of Learning*, gives my personal, and admittedly idiosyncratic, discoveries over the years. I wish I had these gems in my teens. Discoveries, I now find, most adults still seem to have missed.

Of course, I may not have acted on that knowledge, but still it would have been nice to know.

In many cases, knowing then what I know now would have saved me time, money, and heartache; would have enriched me, and given me greater personal freedom.

This second book, on *Money and Wealth*, extracts what I have learned about what it means to have more real wealth and less debt.

Along the way, I've found fascinating answers to key questions:

What is the difference between money and wealth?

Why do people so easily end up living a life in debt?

How can I be aware of con artists picking my pocket?

The publishing imprint I have chosen, The School of Pythagoras, points to the quest for the fundamental nature of Truth.

This series is dedicated to those of you on that quest.

MONEY AND WEALTH

Introduction

Live within your means, never be in debt...
when you get in debt you become a slave.
Therefore I say to you never involve yourself in debt,
and become no man's surety.
Andrew Jackson to his ward, 1833

If you learn one thing only from this little book, then let it be this:

Debt is slavery.

Look at the people around you.

• Many owe money to others.

• A few have money owed to them by others; they never need to owe money to others.

Who is in a better position?

Which person would you rather be—the person who owes money, or the person who never needs to owe money?

Do you want to be the person with DEBTS
(student loans, credit card payments,
mortgages, car payments)?

Or do you want to be the person with ASSETS
(investments, savings,

extra cash on hand)?

Perhaps not all debt is bad. In special cases, a temporary debt can provide value that exceeds the debt. But most people these days live in a state of perpetual debt.

And few realize that others actively try to put people in that state by convincing them that buying now and paying later is a natural part of life.

Charles Lamb, an English essayist, wrote in 1823, "The human species, according to the best theory I can form of it, is composed of two distinct races, the men who borrow, and the men who lend."

The Chinese, one of the oldest civilizations on Earth, have many sayings about debt, including:

• A good debt is not as good as no debt.

• One who restrains his appetites avoids debt.

• Free from debt is free from care.

After thousands of years of history, could the Chinese be onto something?

Around 600 B.C. a Greek writer named Aesop wrote fables to teach children moral lessons. One story is called *The Ant and the Grasshopper.*

> In a field one summer's day, Grasshopper was hopping about, chirping and singing to his heart's content. Ant passed by carrying an ear of corn that she was taking to the nest.
>
> "Why not come and chat with me," said Grasshopper, "instead of working so hard?"
>
> "I am helping to store food for the winter," said Ant, "and I recommend you do the same."
>
> "Why bother about winter?" said Grasshopper. "We have plenty of food right now."
>
> But Ant went on her way and continued working. When winter came Grasshopper had no food and he began dying of hunger. Ant, however, had plenty of corn and grain.
>
> Grasshopper learned a harsh lesson:
>
> *It is best to prepare now for harder times.*

What the story does not reveal is how Grasshopper had spent the summer maxing out his credit cards in clothing stores and shopping malls, ordering video games online, and buying a new car with six years of payments.

And when he went to college, he took out over $100,000 in student loans for his major in a specialized, non-technical field. And the job he landed paid so little he had to live with his parents instead of buying a home and starting a family.

So when winter came, he had nothing to fall back on. And he had creditors at his door threatening him constantly.

We'll talk about credit cards later on. But for now it's just enough to admit:

> *There are people in the world*
> *who benefit from your desire*
> *to have things now and pay later.*

These people may, just may, be willing to convince you that debt is always a good thing.

But there's an old adage, TANSTAAFL (There Ain't No Such Thing As A Free Lunch). Anyone who tries to convince you that something is free is not being honest with you.

Someone always pays, and often you pay in ways you don't see.

How This Little Book Can Help

Most people do not understand economics, money, wealth, credit, debt, inflation, currency, and circulation.

As a result, they are targeted by con artists. Not just con artists in your neighborhood, but con artists on Wall Street and in government (at all levels).

And often these con artists don't realize they are con artists. They think they are doing the right thing.

You probably already know that money gives you more freedom to choose. After studying this little book, you will know how to protect yourself more effectively against the con artists who take advantage of your ignorance and pick your pockets.

This little book simplifies difficult concepts, and it provides practical guidance.

Now for a glimpse into what follows:

> *Chapter 1: What Is Wealth?* explains how wealth and money are not the same thing, and that you can even have wealth without money.

> *Chapter 2: Trade* shows how honorable people, with wealth and the freedom to choose, naturally create free trade.

> *Chapter 3: Jobs* explores how honorable people with wealth and skills naturally create jobs when they are free to choose how to work together.

> *Chapter 4: Government* points to the first legitimate role of any government and suggests what roles government should not adopt in a free society.

> *Chapter 5: Taxes* distinguishes between productive and destructive taxation.

Chapter 6: Money defines the four characteristics of true money and explains the nature of counterfeiting.

Chapter 7: Paper Currency draws a clear line between real money and what symbolically represents real money.

Chapter 8: Banking reveals the origin of institutional lending, and how it can build the wealth of a community.

Chapter 9: Inflation offers a real definition of inflation (hint: it's not "rising prices"), and how con artists actively perpetuate a misunderstanding of what inflation is and how it works.

Chapter 10: A History of U.S. Money shatters some common illusions about the nature of money, coin, paper currency, and banking.

Chapter 11: Credit and Debt offers you a look at how people profit from enslaving you through perpetual debt.

Chapter 12: Investments suggests how you can start protecting your assets and increasing real wealth.

Several chapters end with a special *Deep Dive* section. Where the main text explores topics in an easy-to-understand way, the *Deep Dive* gets into more complex, challenging, and even controversial topics.

For some, it may be best to read the main text first throughout the book, and then later come back to the *Deep Dive* sections.

At the end of the book is a *Money and Wealth* checklist and a recommended reading list. You will also find appendixes that offer details for the more scholarly readers.

The key understandings in this book, faithfully applied, *do* deliver results. You have to experience the results yourself to realize fully the value of this new way of looking at money and wealth.

As we saw in the first book of this series, *Creating Your Life (A Lifetime of Learning, Book 1),* your mind can create blind spots to the truth. When it does, the truth can look crazy and create some anxiety.

Be aware that your mind may rebel against some ideas presented here. The mind creates anxiety when faced with an idea that conflicts with its picture of the world.

Your mind may want to label and categorize these new ideas so that you can dismiss them and avoid anxiety. For example, a mind can avoid looking at a truth when it can label the person expressing that truth as a political progressive, liberal, or conservative.

But truths are truths.

Be thoughtful; do not immediately discount any idea that creates anxiety or makes you feel you must dismiss it as ridiculous or not worth examining.

> *Accepting new truths is not always easy.*
> *But it is worthwhile.*

If you experience some inner conflict or anxiety, take time with the new ideas. Examine your assumptions.

Evaluate why you have them. Be open to new, challenging points of view.

You may discover that you have cherished opinions that you automatically accepted from others. You may want to critically examine those opinions.

When facing an inner anxiety arising from the conflict of ideas, you invite the possibility of enlightened discovery.

So let's begin this marvelous adventure.

Chapter 1

What Is Wealth?

It's not money that makes life better, it's wealth.
You don't have to have a lot of money;
you want wealth.
Richard Maybury, *Early Warning Report,* June/July 2008

What is wealth?

If you answered "Money,"
Bzzzt! Wrong.
Thanks for playing.

Money as it exists today can be a *sign* of wealth. It can be used to *measure or trade* wealth.

But money is not wealth. Knowing the difference can make *all* the difference in how you choose to make a living. And how you choose to view people with wealth and those who want your wealth.

Later, we will talk about what real money is. First, let's look at wealth...

Here's a clue:

> *If governments could create wealth,*
> *they would have no need for taxes.*

Wealth is goods and services—food, clothing, homes, tools, auto repair, plumbing services, literature and the arts, entertainment, personal and professional skills—just about everything that makes life better is wealth.

Money makes *trading* wealth easier. I can use money to specify the value of my professional skills and physical work in relation to the products you are selling.

A monetary value can be placed on goods and services; therefore, money is one method of *measuring* your wealth.

Money can also predict your ability to *acquire* wealth. If you have a wage or salary, you have an idea about what kinds of, and how much, wealth is available to you.

But money itself is not wealth.

Let's break it down...

Imagine three small islands, each with a village of about 100 people:

- Gold Island

- Silver Island

- Iron Island

The people on Gold Island are, by nature, good and ethical people who trust each other. They appear good and are good inside. They all have to work hard just to survive day to day.

They live by a high standard of ethics.

The people on Iron Island are just the opposite. They are bandits and pirates: dishonest, ruthless, manipulative, selfish, and dangerous. They appear bad and are bad on the inside.

In other words, they are openly bad, and do not care who knows it. They form thieving bands that believe in "honor among thieves," mostly. They do not want to work hard to survive. They enjoy taking from others who do have to work hard.

The people on Silver Island are a mix. They are inherently both good and bad, and everything in between. Some of them can appear good but be bad on the inside. Some of them are good on both the outside and inside in some situations, but not in other situations. They can work hard to survive but cut ethical corners when the opportunity arises.

Let's first focus on the people of Gold Island.

Each day in order to survive, each person on Gold Island has to catch one fish, get one coconut, and drink two gallons of water. It takes twelve hours of work each day on average for each person to get the food to survive.

Everyone barely manages to live.

One day, one man, let's call him Tor, gets an idea. Tor labors extra hard to get an extra fish, an extra coconut, and extra water. He now has enough for a free day.

He spends that day inventing a fishing pole. He practices with the fishing pole until he develops the ability (the skill) to use it. The next day he catches ten fish.

This man, this inventor—using his imagination and creativity, and sacrificing for his vision—just created wealth. Specifically, labor-saving wealth.

Labor-saving wealth is created out of two things:

1. A valuable labor-saving idea

2. The work necessary to manifest that idea

*Wealth is created out of
imagination and work.*

*Labor-saving wealth often saves people time,
freeing them from mere survival.
Wealth has inherent value to you or others.*

Notice that money is not necessary to create wealth. If
you have good ideas or good skills, you can create wealth
out of your work, or out of the work of others.

On Gold Island, both the fish *and* the ability
to catch fish are actual wealth.

Because our inventor, Tor, can now catch
ten fish in the time it used to take to catch
one fish, he has more free time. (Fishing
used to take four hours; it's hard to catch a
fish in the ocean with your hands.)

He and his wife Sophia can now go several
days without having to fish (if they salt the
fish).

In fact, Sophia doesn't have to fish or get
coconuts anymore. Tor is skilled at getting
coconuts (two hours on average to get one).
His wife is strong, and willing to walk the six
hours, round trip, to get enough water for
them both.

Meanwhile, in his free time, Tor is fixing the
roof and building an additional room, since
Sophia is newly pregnant.

One day Sophia has a good idea. She's been thinking of ways to get coconuts more quickly. Throwing rocks at coconuts works sometimes when they are overly ripe. But often, coconuts grow higher than her husband can throw. And the ones that are ripe will not always drop when hit by a hand-thrown rock.

Sophia dreams up the idea of a slingshot.

Working together in their *spare time*, they create the slingshot. They both practice until they have the skill to knock down ten coconuts in the time it once took to knock down one.

Tor and Sophia now have even more wealth, more time to do other things.

Wealth is one of the most important things anyone can create.

> *Wealth frees people from drudgery.*
> *Wealth grants time to do other work,*
> *or time to play.*
> *Wealth is essentially good.*

In other words,

Wealth grants freedom.

There are other kinds of wealth.

Ver is a great storyteller. He can gather the community together around a bonfire and begin telling tales of old.

Tales of monsters and heroes, and stories of great passions, both hateful and loving.

Ver has the extraordinary ability to voice many characters. He can act out the parts. Villagers from miles away will come to hear his stories.

Ver enriches everyone's life with sorrows and tears, and laughter and joy, and all the passions his characters experience.

His tales provide moral examples of what happens to those who do right. And what happens to those who do wrong.

And because he is such a unique and wonderful storyteller, he becomes known as Ver the Great Storyteller.

The villagers are willing to give him food and drink and other goods in order for him to keep telling his stories.

People who are free from constant labor may write a song or a book, or may paint a picture that someone else wants. These provide pleasure. They may not create something that saves time and labor, but they may still create something that others want.

Something others value. Something that enhances their lives.

Great music, great art, great literature, great storytelling: these are all kinds of wealth that, when created with noble ideals, can uplift, improve, and generally better people.

Leisure-enhancing wealth.

When someone like Ver the Great Storyteller creates something that others value, they have created wealth. Not necessarily labor-saving wealth, but it is still a kind of wealth. It has value, or at least someone sees value in it.

Wealth has intrinsic value;
that is, wealth has value in and of itself.

Ten salted fish have value when others know that they have to work four hours to catch a fish. Even if no one else wants the fish I have, I can eat it. It has *intrinsic value*, not just an official value that some authority, like government, declares it to have.

The same is true of gold or silver. If someone has it, they can make jewelry out of it. The value is *intrinsic*, in the thing itself.

People use their imagination and develop skills to create, *out of thin air* in a sense, things with intrinsic value. Wealth. Both labor-saving wealth, and leisure-enhancing wealth.

Like debt, wealth is a habit.
Wealthy people realize
that life is more than luck.

Life is action. Life is imagination.
Active, hardworking people create wealth.

As imaginative and hardworking people create wealth, they often create more than they need.

What can they do with their extra wealth?

Deep Dive: Logical Fallacies

Some things are believed because they are demonstrably true. But many things are believed because they are consistent with a widely held vision of the world—and this vision is accepted as a substitute for facts.
Thomas Sowell, *Economic Facts and Fallacies*

Never underestimate the difficulty of changing false beliefs by facts.
Henry Rosovsky, *The University: An Owner's Manual*

First, a question: Can you name any logical fallacies without Googling them? If not, you may be prey to con artists who can offer you an apparent truth that is in fact a lie.

The most common and known include:

- *Ad Hominem:* Rather than addressing the argument, the person's character is attacked. "Well, you know that she is from Texas, so you can't trust what she says."

- *Straw Man:* Rather than addressing the argument, something unrelated is attacked. "I bet you think we can solve all of our environmental problems by driving electric cars."

- *Circular Reasoning:* A circular argument assumes what's being argued. "The Bible is true because it says that it's true."

When it comes to economics, there are several logical fallacies worth considering, as presented by Thomas Sowell, the pre-eminent scholar of economic sanity:

- *The Zero-Sum Fallacy:* The belief that economic transactions always mean that when one person gains something, another person must lose something.

  This is the biggest fallacy many people commit when talking about economics. Chapter 2 on Trade goes into some detail on how free trade can actually create wealth and everyone involved benefits.

  Listen when someone makes an argument about economics. Do they assume there are only winners and losers? It's an easy mistake to make.

  Most people, especially young people in college, have yet to experience how wealth is created, and understand how free trade can be a most valuable activity.

  Free trade occurs most often between two people. The transaction benefits both, since both will only choose to trade if they feel they are getting more value than what they are giving.

However, distortions begin to occur when government gets involved. Government suddenly becomes the third party to the transaction. The two parties to the trade may no longer be free to choose, and, in fact, the third party, government, may *create* through force a winner and a loser.

When government fallaciously assumes a zero-sum standard, then government uses that as an excuse to *create* a zero-sum standard. And in the process government may actually create a *negative-sum* activity, by taking money from the two parties in order to force both to trade the way government wants them to trade.

- *The Fallacy of Composition:* The belief that what is true of a part is also true for the whole.

You may be at a football game, and in order to get a better view you decide to stand up. Yes, you get a better view, but what if everyone wants a better view? If everyone stands up, nobody gets a better view. What is true for one is not true for all.

When people claim that government spending benefits the economy, looked at in part, yes, it appears to be true. If government subsidizes corn growers, yes, the corn growers benefit, they get more money and they spend more money.

But if that money remained in the hands of the taxpayers, it's usually the case that those taxpayers would also have more money and spend more money. When government taxes and spends, it creates a negative-sum process, reducing incentives for businesses and taxpayers to generate economic activity.

- *The Chess-Pieces Fallacy:* The belief that human beings are just like chess pieces that can be moved around strategically to enhance the economy.

This fallacy is common among professors and academics who love to plan without having to directly experience the results of their planning.

Any medical doctor will tell you that it's one thing to have go to medical school and learn the theories; it's quite another thing to go into clinical practice for many years. The doctor learns that theories don't apply equally to individuals, that with experience a doctor acquires professional judgment that tells her how a certain treatment will not work for one patient in the same way as another.

When you view people as chess pieces, you first commit the indignity of turning them in objects. But more telling, you take away choice.

Humans have their own preferences, values, and plans that can conflict with social experiments. Government may spend billions on social experiments that fail simply because people don't respond as the chess pieces that social experimenters expect.

And the experimenters don't acknowledge the fallacy *because* they make their livelihood off of those experiments.

- *The Open-Ended Fallacy*: The belief that resources are not limited.

  Who is against health? No one. So doesn't it make sense that government get involved in insuring health for everyone? And no matter how much government can do to promote health, can't government do more? *Shouldn't* government do more?

  What the purveyors of this fallacy fail to see is that resources are limited and, therefore, with limited resources come trade-offs. Resources can have more than one kind of use.

  When you take choice away from individuals and mandate a kind of cookie-cutter approach to health spending for everyone, many find themselves having their money spent on services that don't need or prioritize. People may rather spend that money on something else deemed more important.

  If I am forced into a government health plan and taxed, I have less money that may go to help my children in another way, a way that I would have chosen for my family if the choice still rested with me.

This list barely touches the number of important economic fallacies that are commonly on display in public discourse. I heartily recommend Thomas Sowell's books, which are full of research revealing the facts that blow up so much of what is believed that is not true.

And don't be surprised if you mention Sowell to a friend and that friend disparages Sowell's character. They will not have read his facts, and must attack him personally to avoid having their myths messed with.

Chapter 2

Trade

*The principle of a free trade is founded in justice,
and beneficial to the whole.*
Edmund Burke,
letter to Thomas Burgh, Esq, Jan. 1, 1780

Extra wealth provides the opportunity for trade.

One woman on Gold Island, Kendra, has a husband who works extra hard to help his family survive and give his wife extra time. She uses that extra time to create new kinds of blankets and clothes that last longer and keep people warmer.

Sophia likes what she sees and begins to trade coconuts and fish for Kendra's blankets and clothes. They agree that one fish equals one blanket, and that two fish equals one set of clothes.

Pretty soon, other people see Kendra's and Sophia's families prospering. They also get ideas to create and trade for other items.

Free trade and wealth creation
are intimately linked.

When the environment allows the freedom for people to apply their ingenuity, a natural creative instinct arises.

People create.

And when they get rewarded for their creations, an inner drive is strengthened to create more, to experiment, to innovate.

They are willing to work for their creations.

The work may be hard, but people who are fired up by a creative idea often work harder than most, late into the night, driven by that creative fire.

Furthermore, when people see something they cannot create themselves, they are willing to trade their labor to acquire the product desired. And both win. They both trade for something they value more.

Sophia sees the blankets and clothes that Kendra creates. Sophia knows that Kendra has special skills for weaving. Kendra also knows that Sophia has special skills using a slingshot to get coconuts.

They both are willing to trade their separate labors to get products that would take much more work and time to create for themselves. So both get value.

Sophia has extra coconuts. The coconuts she gives to Kendra are not as valuable to her as the blankets and clothing.

The same is true for Kendra. She values Sophia's coconuts more than the extra blankets and clothing she worked hard to create.

So they trade. Freely.

And both are enriched.

Both get more value. Both are happier with what they have after the trade.

The desire to create and the freedom to choose provide an environment for trade, an environment that enriches individuals. But even more is now possible.

Good people who think beyond themselves, who think of their community, begin to have bigger creative ideas.

Soon there is a thriving economy on Gold Island. And more people have more leisure time. More people begin to create.

Tor's neighbor, Alex, has an idea.

Alex sees everyone setting off each day and walking for hours to get water. He notices that the source of the water is higher than the village.

He gets the idea of building a simple wooden trough. The trough would take advantage of gravity and transport water to their village.

He brings this idea to Tor and they devise a plan.

Using Tor's fishing pole and Sophia's slingshot, some islanders will be assigned to catch fish, and others assigned to knock down coconuts. And some others will get water.

All this work will free up the time for a couple dozen laborers. Those laborers, supervised by Alex and Tor, would begin building the wooden trough.

It would take time, but the labor would benefit everyone. Nobody likes walking and carrying so much water.

Inspired by the vision that Alex and Tor present to the community, everyone chooses the role that is best for them. Days go by, and finally the trough is finished.

Water begins flowing to the village.

The trough creates even more wealth, but this time the entire village benefits. No one needs to spend hours each day walking to get water.

And a community is born based on labor, choice, ingenuity, and trade. The entire community shares in the wealth.

All without money.

It's crucial to understand that *free trade* is good *only* when both sides have a choice in the exchange.

Trade happens when all participants in the trade feel they have more after the trade than before.

True trade works only when there exists choice.

When nobody forces the trade,
then both sides get the value they seek.

Kendra will only trade with Sophia if Kendra believes that what Sophia offers is of equal or greater value to Kendra's work, and to the things that she herself produces.

The same goes for Sophia.

The members of the community get together to build the trough, or support those who do, because they all benefit. They all see how they will have greater wealth after the trough is built.

And since everyone lives on Gold Island, there is no fraud, no lying, and no stealing. No desire for crime of any sort.

Of course, these virtues are not held by the people on one of the neighboring small islands, Iron Island.

The people on Iron Island have a very different view of the world. (We will see how this plays out later, when we talk about the need for a government.)

With the idea of trade comes the idea of *trade-offs*.

> *Understanding trade-offs is crucial to understanding different economic systems.*

Suppose I love crafting warm coats, which people only tend to want during three cold months out of the year. By choosing to do what I love—be a crafter of warm coats—I must accept that there is a trade-off.

The trade-off is this: I get to do what I love, *but* I may have to go without trade (or with reduced trading value) the rest of the year.

I accept responsibility for understanding that there is a trade-off with my chosen craft.

But the idea of trade-offs extends further.

If the community chooses to engage in a free trade economy, they accept the fact that people have to work to participate in the community. People have to have something to trade, either by creating something themselves, or by agreeing to help produce something that another person has created.

In other words, as trade increases and people choose a free trade economy, the door opens to another beneficial activity that helps individuals and the whole community—jobs.

Deep Dive: What Is Economics?

Economics is the study of the use of scarce resources which have alternative uses.

Many people do not want to admit that they can't have everything. Or that some people should not have everything.

It's true that all of us, *all of us*, no matter our income or social status, have desires that exceed what we can comfortably afford.

In the United States, people who have Xboxes and smartphones, resources that exceed the imagination of people in many countries, are regarded as poor.

You know you are beginning to understand economics once you grasp that there is never enough to satisfy everyone.

In short, this is what is meant by *scarcity*.

Scarcity defines human history. No matter how much wealth is created, there is still scarcity. The economic system doesn't matter. Scarcity rules all.

Productivity concerns decisions on what to do with scarce resources, decisions made about using land, labor, capital, and other scarce resources.

The key to keep in mind is: Every resource has multiple uses. Think of petroleum. What do you get from it? Gasoline, yes, but also heating oil and asphalt and plastics, and... the list goes on.

How much of each resource should be allocated to each of its possible uses? Who should decide? Who could possibly *know* enough to decide.

That is the basic question of economics: How do we most efficiently and effectively use scarce resources?

People propose many kinds of economic models in order to make those decisions. History shows what happens with each of those models.

No model appears perfect, but some cause more misery than others because of the inefficient and ineffective use of scarce resources.

Please don't make the mistake of thinking that economics is about money. No, it's about goods and services. Productivity.

As stated by Thomas Sowell in *Basic Economics*, "It is not money but the volume of goods and services which determines whether a country is poverty stricken or prosperous."

Chapter 3

Jobs

Don't be afraid to give your best to what seemingly are small jobs. Every time you conquer one it makes you that much stronger. If you do the little jobs well, the big ones will tend to take care of themselves.
Dale Carnegie,
from *How to Win Friends and Influence People*

Extra wealth and trade provide the opportunity for jobs.

Our inventor, Tor, realizes that he could put the wealth he has already created to work and increase the amount of wealth he has to trade.

He makes his neighbor, Jay, an offer. Tor will teach his neighbor how to fish with his fishing pole and let him fish for ten fish each day, five days each week.

In exchange, each day Tor gets six fish and his neighbor keeps four. They both see this as fair, since Tor invented the fishing pole and taught his neighbor a skill.

Tor has created a *job* for Jay, a kind of working *trade*.

Jay trades his time and effort for learning a skill and receiving extra fish. More fish than he could catch on his own.

As a result, Tor is now busy with a *business*, a *free enterprise*.

Why free?

Because Tor is free to sell and trade what he wants, and Jay is free to trade his labor for what he wants.

> *Both men benefit from Jay's job.*
> *Tor gets six fish each day*
> *from his neighbor's labors.*
>
> *Jay acquires a skill for life.*
> *Jay gets four fish in the time*
> *he used to get one fish.*

Notice that trade does not necessarily involve money. An exchange takes place that both people value.

And there is one more critical thing to understand about this kind of working trade.

>*Working trade is a choice*
>*that benefits all involved.*

Tor and Jay both prosper. Soon Tor invites others to fish for him, creating more jobs and allowing more and more people to save time.

Meanwhile, Tor's wife, Sophia, teaches others to use the slingshot in exchange for some of the coconuts they knock down.

Tor and Sophia begin building more wealth as they become *employers*.

Community and Jobs

Free choice and jobs create more of a community, as well as create the possibility of culture.

The community is going strong.

It turns out that a small number of people in the village are naturally good at fishing, so they fish for the community by trading those fish for other products, or *goods*, and services. (I will give you two fish if you wash these clothes for me.)

Other people are good at using the slingshot to get coconuts and trade them for other goods and services. It's the same with

blankets and clothing and hats and baskets and shoes and jewelry and spears.

Soon more people are creating an increasing variety of goods and services. They are building *specialized* skills.

If someone does not want to join in with the community, that's OK.

They can continue their own fishing without a fishing pole and knocking down their own coconuts without a slingshot.

Since water comes to the community, the community may decide to let that person have the water. But that person still has a choice to participate in the community.

All kinds of things now begin to happen, simply because of:

— The ingenuity of individuals

— The willingness of others to learn a skill

— The labor of all parties involved

— Their freedom to choose

Trades and Crafts

Originally, people who labored with their hands—such as carpenters, bricklayers, plumbers, and others engaged in manual labor—were said to have a *trade.*

Why?

Because they would steadily acquire skills that allowed them to *trade* skilled labor for products or money. Being a skilled tradesman meant having some value to offer others.

Other people focused on developing skills in crafting products, such as furniture, jewelry, tools, sculpture, music, and other things that people wanted. They became *craftsmen.*

Their skills allow them to specialize in *crafting* products that few can do for themselves.

These people made themselves valuable by pioneering and increasing their value, their ability to provide something others would trade for.

> *Having skills is having wealth.*
> *Having skills that others value,*
> *that others will trade goods or money for,*
> *is having wealth.*

Skilled people are wealthy people. And if they are free to choose their skills, their trades, their crafts, and they are free to apply their imagination to go beyond the boundaries—they are free to invent themselves and create their own new, specialized jobs.

They create new wealth.

Jobs offer people who are not personally creative or entrepreneurial a way to participate in a free trade economy.

The trade-off may be that they have to labor in new ways, either physically or mentally. But they can acquire new skills and increase their sense of personal value.

Of course, now you are thinking, "Yes, that's all well and good. But in the real world not everyone is good and honest like those on Gold Island."

What happens when you have to deal with human nature? With people who are not so good and honest? With people who choose to exploit and abuse workers?

Good question.

Deep Dive: Good Intentions

Economics is not about how to make money, personal finance, or playing the stock market. Economics is about how decisions are made and the consequences of those decisions.

What resources are available?

How do decisions affect how those resources are allocated?

Do the decisions raise or lower the standard of living of people as a whole?

At its core, economics is about understanding the law of *cause and effect.* Understanding how decisions lead to certain results and ensuring that one must look at the facts to determine that the results are connected to the right causes.

If you are getting results you do not desire, to correct the course, you must clearly grasp what the true causes are. Not causes dictated by a certain political, economic, or philosophical vision. Causes dictated by facts.

It's important to distinguish between *incentives* created by economic decision and the *goals* of economic decisions. This distinction allows for seeing how consequences matter more than intentions.

Some will claim that a decision based on a moral economic goal is somehow more important than a decision based on creating incentives. But history is factually full of good economic intentions leading to disastrous consequences due to a lack of understanding what incentives are being created.

Read articles on Venezuela's economic disaster, in a country with incredible natural resources, incredible opportunities for wealth. Venezuela's economy, based on a moral vision of what's good for the people, has allowed the leader's family to become billionaires while the people starve.

Economic principles are not a matter of opinion any more than the basic principles of biology, chemistry, or physics.

A non-ideological, that is, non-visionary, understanding of economics is important because economic decisions have real-world consequences.

When first responders arrive at a natural disaster, they know that resources are scarce. They know that there are only so many medical personnel, only so many specialists, and so many antibiotics and medical devices.

Experienced responders do not make decisions based on an ideology of "this person's social standing puts them ahead of others." They must quickly determine who needs the most urgent care, who will probably die despite extraordinary efforts because of the heavy nature of their wounds.

They apply The Law of Economy. Since time and resources are scarce, each medical professional must determine how that time and those resources must be allocated for the best overall result.

And so they must deal in trade-offs. Yes, this decision will mean that one person dies. But time is better spent so several others may live.

Economics is about right decisions, recognizing trade-offs, and making the most of the options available.

Chapter 4

Government

If men were angels,
no government would be necessary.
James Madison,
from *Federalist No. 51*

True business is based on choice. When the threat of force exists, you have something else.

What happens when people and communities exist that do not have honesty and integrity?

Who cannot be trusted?

Let's talk about Iron Island and how the people on that Island are different from those on Gold Island.

Gold Island vs. Iron Island

The people on Gold Island each have a moral conscience. They behave in such a way that they do not seek to gain something at the expense of others. They do what they do for themselves and their loved ones without causing conscious harm.

> *A good, healthy culture instills a moral conscience.*

However, the people on Iron Island do *not* each have a moral conscience. They take what they want from others without regard for the harm they cause. In fact, many enjoy the harm they cause others. They delight in exercising power.

> Zahn is a pirate. He is greedy and strong, and he enjoys taking what he wants from others on Iron Island. He forces others to fish for him and get him water.

> Zahn has some fellow bandits who also enjoy taking and hurting. Since they are not as strong as Zahn, he rules. He rewards those who follow his rules and punishes those who don't.

> Zahn and his fellows rule by force and whim. The rules can change every day, if he chooses. Anyone that questions his rules can try to kill him. But they know if they fail, he will kill them.

One day, Zahn's son Zeb tells him about another island he and his buddies found while out on a raft. The island had many people with plenty of fish, coconuts, and exotic clothes—Gold Island.

With a gleam in his eye, he persuades his father to let him take a pirate crew there at night, sneak in, and take all they can without waking anyone.

Zahn laughs and agrees.

The next day, the people on Gold Island wake up to discover that the pirates from Iron Island had paddled over the waters in the dark of night.

They had sneaked into the village and stole stores of fish and coconuts, boxes of clothes and blankets, and even some fishing poles and slingshots.

The people of Gold Island decide to take some kind of action to protect themselves and their wealth.

People with a healthy moral conscience *govern* their own behavior. The people of Gold Island each have a healthy moral conscience.

> *They are intrinsically governed—*
> *governed from the inside.*

People without a healthy moral conscience do not govern their own behavior. The people of Iron Island do not have a healthy moral conscience.

> *They need to be extrinsically governed— governed from the outside.*

As a community forms, members of that community soon discover they need to govern the behavior of outsiders who are a threat to their community.

When the people of Gold Island awaken to what the pirates of Iron Island have done, they awaken to a new danger. All their labor has gone to people who do not earn their keep, people who are simply willing to take what they want.

What to do?

Several leading thinkers in the community, like Sophia and Alex, come up with a plan.

The village is now becoming more complex and specialized. Different people have different specialized work they do to contribute to themselves and to their community.

For example, those good at fishing, fish. Those good with a slingshot collect coconuts. Those good at making blankets, make blankets. They keep what they make, and when someone wants what they have, they trade.

The people love how their lives work. But they need protection from those who would take what they produce.

So they come up with a plan for each person to contribute something to a small group of people who will lead the community's defense and protect the community against theft.

They form a new kind of institution, a new kind of job. They choose people to specialize in governing the bad behavior of the outsiders, who become *guardians*.

The people in the community grant these people the right to exercise *force* on outsiders who engage in bad behavior.

However, some people worry about giving guardians such power. They want everyone to agree and be clear on what "bad behavior" means.

So... what is that bad behavior?

They come up with the two laws:

1) Do all you have agreed to do, and

2) Do not encroach on other persons or their property.

In other words, they agree on laws that require people to avoid fraud and lying, and also stealing and physically hurting others.

People who do not follow these laws are acting outside the law.

They are outlaws.

So certain members are now paid, not to produce any wealth directly, but to stand guard, to protect the wealth created by members of the community, and to apply force when needed.

Soon a small number of people form a local council to coordinate these activities. They propose plans. Everyone in the community discusses these plans and decides on the best courses of action.

They have formed a small *government*, supported voluntarily by the community.

The main purpose of a government for a community based on choice and free trade is simple: to govern externally some people's bad behavior in order to protect members of the community and their property.

What is the difference between a business and a government?

A business is based on choice.
People choose to trade or not to trade.

Properly understood, a business is distinguished by *choice*, the freedom to choose. No one is required to buy.

A government passes laws and exercises force to make sure people comply with the laws.

A government is based on force.

When the laws created are good and applied equally to everyone, including those who make the laws, then the government is good.

On Gold Island, the rule is *Equal justice before the law.*

Everyone is equally held accountable for obeying the laws. The laws are written, and everyone agrees on the meaning of the written laws. Nobody can make up laws on a whim, out of thin air.

On Iron Island, the opposite is true: *Might makes right.*

On Iron Island, it's survival of the fittest and most ruthless. Any wealth produced comes from slave labor.

The most ruthless and powerful bandits, like Zahn, power their way to the top. They make the rules (laws), and if they choose to change the rules, they do.

Some leaders can change the laws every day, or apply different laws to different people. They create laws on a whim, out of their own heads.

The people on Gold Island want to preserve their free society. So they have to do something to protect it from people who do not care for the rules of a free society.

They create a limited government.

There is a significant trade-off that comes with forming a government. Government has the power to exercise force.

On Gold Island, there is no concern about people abusing their power.

The people of Iron Island, of course, are expected to abuse power.

However, on Silver Island there would be concern about the potential abuse of power. That is the trade-off. If you have government, you are giving people the power to coerce.

And people being people, they will be tempted to abuse their power.

One thing is clear.

A small and limited government
helps keep a community healthy, wealthy, and free.

Deep Dive: A Note About Rights

People like to talk today about the *right* to food, the *right* to a home, the *right* to healthcare, and so on. They say government must provide these.

To most people, these are obvious rights. How can you object to them? Anyone with compassion should support these fundamental human rights.

In the short view, these seem to be praiseworthy goals.

> *But looking beyond the short view,*
> *you discover these so-called rights*
> *can cause great harm.*

Not all rights are the same.

The Declaration of Independence announced for the first time that certain natural rights supersede man-made law. The right to life, liberty, and the pursuit of happiness. (Magna Carta started the process but did not fully articulate this distinction.)

> *People had the natural right*
> *to be **free from constraints**.*

The main idea here is that governments should exist to provide freedom from constraints. Therefore, a government should be limited (since the inherent nature of government is to *constrain* through force of law).

What then is the role of government designed for a free people? To protect people equally so they can be free to choose how to live their lives.

Limited governments protect people from criminal violence, and from criminal fraud. They do not apply force except in these limited categories.

So why not have governments enforce the rights to food, homes, and healthcare?

Because these are not natural rights.

They are rights to *commodities*.

In other words, from a Gold Island perspective...

> *By asserting a right to food,*
> *someone else is **constrained***
> *to provide that food.*

> *By asserting a right to a home,*
> *someone else is **constrained***
> *to provide that home.*

> *By asserting a right to healthcare,*
> *someone else is **constrained***
> *to provide that healthcare.*

Therefore, commodity rights are directly opposed to the basic natural rights of life, liberty, and the pursuit of happiness—the right to be free from constraints.

And therefore are directly opposed to free trade.

Other people have to work (be enslaved) to provide these commodities.

You cannot have it both ways. However, anyone emotionally attached to commodity rights will provide all kinds of rationalizations to justify them.

> *History shows time and again that*
> *rights to commodities lead to human slavery*
> *and the collapse of a civil society.*

People who do not understand basic economics only look at the immediate results of an action, law, or policy. They do not look at long-term consequences, or to the impact those actions, laws, or policies may have on other groups.

Furthermore, from a Silver Island perspective,

government may have a role protecting a community's ability to access clean water, healthy food, and proper shelter. These can be protected under the Two Laws.

Even a safety net for emergency healthcare can be provided by government.

However, that's quite different from saying that people have a right to them without work or some way to earn what they receive.

One final thought: Government is not the only way to get things done.

But that is a discussion for another book. See *Law and Liberty (A Lifetime of Learning, Book 9)*.

For now, it's enough to understand that "rights to commodities" is how the pirates on Iron Island view the world.

One group of people labors to create wealth, and another simply takes the fruit of that labor—through force.

Side Notes

Note 1

The Two Laws mentioned in this chapter, laws essential for a civilized society, were first formulated by writer Richard Maybury in his book *Whatever Happened to Justice?*

Note 2

Businesses in a free market that engage in genuine capitalism do not constrain people to buy their products and services the way governments can.

When businesses get in bed with governments to exercise force through monopolies and coercive trades, we are not talking about free markets and capitalism anymore.

These businesses are exercising the power of government force to get what they want.

At best these businesses are engaging in *crony-capitalism*. Free markets have nothing to do with their activities.

Remember: Crony-capitalism is not true capitalism.

Chapter 5

Taxes

*Taxation is the price which civilized communities pay
for the opportunity of remaining civilized.*
Albert Bushnell Hart,
from *Actual Government As Applied Under American
Conditions* (1903)

Taxes can be good or bad.

When governments tax, they use the threat of coercive power to take something of value from people. Sometimes the term *voluntary* is used to describe legitimate taxation.

But there is nothing voluntary about what happens when someone refuses to pay the tax.

Taxation always comes with the implied or direct threat of force: confiscation of property, prison, and in rare cases lethal force. There's a reason why special agents of the Internal Revenue Service are authorized to carry concealed weapons.

Normally, when the threat of force is used to take something of value, we call it robbery. But when governments do it, with or without consent, we call it taxation.

In the best case, the people who are being taxed get a say over who gets taxed, and how that tax revenues are used.

On Gold Island, the people support the guardians and the local council, who protect everyone from the bandits from Iron Island.

Everyone helps with the support. Everyone benefits.

Taxes are good when everyone contributes,
and everyone benefits from
how the taxes are used.

Taxes on Gold Island are good taxes.

The bandits on Iron Island think differently. Zahn and his followers simply take what they want, as much as they want, from whomever they want.

They make people catch fish, and then they take all the fish they want. They leave just enough so the fishers can survive and catch more fish.

They call that "collecting taxes." Of course, when someone does not pay their taxes, the consequences are bad.

Are they acting like a government?

Yes. They use the threat of force to take what they want, and threat of force is the distinguishing characteristic of government.

Businesses like those that have developed on Gold Island trade through choice. They do not exercise force; they exercise simple *persuasion*. (Not the manipulative kind.)

In other words, governments force; businesses persuade.

Bad government takes without rules, unequally, without regard for those they take from.

Bad government does not lead to a healthy, civil community.

Not surprisingly, Zahn and his buddies don't care about a healthy, civil community. All they care about is satisfying their own greedy desires.

Therefore, the government on Iron Island is clearly bad. And taxes on Iron Island are bad taxes.

But what about the people on Silver Island?

The people on Gold Island are naturally good. Those on Iron Island are naturally bad.

Silver Island people are different. They are both good and bad, and mixed. Some have come from Gold Island and are openly good. Some have come from Iron Island and are openly bad.

But some from Iron Island appear good and hide their badness. And the rest who are born on Silver Island do not realize how they've been influenced by Iron Island.

Tor and Sophia on Gold Island have a daughter, Jade. She has a friend on Silver Island and ends up moving there and staying with her friend.

Zahn's son, Zeb, also moves to Silver Island, but nobody knows he comes from Iron Island. Zeb has lots of charm, good looks, and a great smile. He is a smooth talker.

He knows how to look good and hide his bad intentions.

Zeb and Jade meet and begin dating. They are both interested in the activities of the local council and having nice things.

Zeb slowly corrupts Jade's thinking about how the Silver Island government should use power, although she does not realize what he is doing. What he says makes so much sense.

For example, Zeb introduces the idea that more should be taken from some people, and other people shouldn't have to pay taxes at all. In essence, Zeb thinks people should be treated unequally before the law.

Jade begins to think he's right, even though, at first, she feels uncomfortable with the idea. Zeb persuades her to get elected to the local council. She does.

He also teaches her how to be a smooth talker.

The people who govern Silver Island are smooth talkers. They know how to use language to fool others and sometimes even fool themselves.

They can talk themselves and others into believing that Good is Bad and Bad is Good.

How this misuse of language works is more fully explored in two other books in this series:

Language and Rhetoric: (A Lifetime of Learning, Book 7)

Law and Liberty: (A Lifetime of Learning, Book 9)

Taxes on Production and Consumption

Generally speaking, a government can tax what people produce (wealth) or they can tax what people consume (purchase or trade).

A tax on production means taking a portion of the wealth that is created. Let's say a government has a 10% wealth tax. Then for every ten fish caught, the government gets one. For every ten baskets created, the government gets one.

A tax on consumption means taking a portion of what is purchased or traded. If you buy ten fish, the government gets one. If you buy ten baskets, the government gets one.

You can already see that in a free trade economy where only the wealth created is traded, problems will arise when a government wants to tax either through consumption or production.

We'll see in the chapter on *Money* how this issue is resolved.

Production and consumption taxes can be either good or bad depending on how they are applied.

Let's list the characteristics of both good taxes and bad taxes.

And keep in mind that exceptions are easy to imagine. An exception does not invalidate the characterization. The discipline comes in applying exceptions rarely, transparently, and with right discrimination.

Characteristics of Good Taxes:

- Everyone contributes in some way

- Everyone benefits from how the tax is used

- If the tax benefits a smaller portion of the people, only those people pay the tax

- The people taxed have a real say in who taxes, who gets taxed, and the amount of the tax

- People are able to keep a majority of what they produce

- People who make a living off of taxes (government workers, for example) do not pay taxes out of that income (which helps keep clear who are the ones creating wealth to pay taxes, and who are the ones living off of that wealth without creating it)

Characteristics of Bad Taxes:

- The tax allows some people to take without a sense of obligation or indebtedness

- People benefit from taxes who do not pay the tax

- Some smaller groups benefit from a tax while others who do not benefit pay for the tax

- People have no real say in who taxes, who gets taxed, and the amount of the tax

- People are taxed a majority of what they produce (turning people into serfs or slaves)

• People who get paid out of tax money pay taxes out of that money (giving the appearance that there is no difference between wealth creators and wealth consumers)

You are probably thinking, "Wait a minute. I can already think of exceptions to this."

What about a basket weaver? How can a basket weaver help the guardians like the fisher, who can provide food?

What about someone who can't work?

Shouldn't taxes be used to help them?

Good questions.

Questions about someone who can't work will be answered more fully in another book. For now, think about what bad things can happen when the threat of force is used to take from one person and to give to another.

When does using the threat of force, even for what the government thinks is good, become similar to what the bandits on Iron Island do?

Think about the smooth talkers on Silver Island.

People can talk you into believing the threat of force is a good thing, and then they use that threat of force for their own benefit.

Or for the benefit of their friends.

George Washington said:

> *"Government is not reason, it is not eloquence;*
> *it is force! Like fire, it is a dangerous servant*
> *and a fearful master."*

When you use the threat of force, limits should be placed on it.

What limits?

We will explore the answers to this question in *Law and Liberty (A Lifetime of Learning, Book 9).*

For now let's keep things simple and focus on the questions about the basket weaver and the fisher.

These questions lead us to our next topic:

Money.

Deep Dive: Who Pays Taxes?

Generally speaking, there are two kinds of people when thinking of taxes: 1) Those paying taxes, and 2) Those who live off the taxes paid.

People in the first category have their own private businesses or work for a private business.

People in the second category work in public service; for example, as military, firefighters, police, and for agencies that perform particular non-first responder roles, such as the U.S. Geological Survey and the Environmental Protection Agency.

These are *not* moral categories. You may have good and bad people in both.

The distinction drawn here is simple: If you have any kind of government agency sending you a check, or, if you work for a company whose income is completely dependent on government funding, you do not pay taxes.

But some argue that even though their income comes from government, they in fact *do* pay taxes.

Well, no. Not really. Sure, government sends you tax forms and applies sales taxes and other kinds of taxes to the money you have.

But those who are really paying your taxes are taxpayers.

Remember, government can't create wealth. If it could, it would have no need for taxes. Government can only tax wealth. And since government can't create wealth, it cannot tax people who do not create wealth.

Even if they have an income, spend money, and fill out tax forms.

The fact that so many people fail to understand this distinction is why so many people do not have a realistic, grounded understanding of economics.

Chapter 6

Money

*"Specie [gold and silver coin] is
the most perfect medium
because it will preserve its own level;
because, having intrinsic and universal value,
it can never die in our hands."*
Thomas Jefferson,
letter to John W. Eppes, Nov. 6, 1813

What is money?

In the best sense, money is anything that people agree to use as:

1) *A unit of account*

2) *A medium of exchange*

3) *A store of value*

4) *A unit of deferred payment.*

Historically, precious metals, mainly gold and silver, best fulfill all four functions. Everyone on Gold Island wants gold and silver (as do the people on Silver Island and Iron Island).

Why do gold and silver work best as money?

Let's break down the four functions of good money:

1. A unit of account

On Gold Island, how many fish equal one woven basket?

What if the fisher thinks the basket is not worth two fish, but agrees that it's worth more than one?

What if the basket weaver does not need fish, but the person wanting the basket has only fish to trade?

You can see the problem.

> The basket weaver wants several things, but not fish. The fisher would then have to go to other people and make trades for things the basket weaver wants. Then after much work

and several trades, the fisher can trade these items for baskets.

Now... let's say that the local council begins to create standard gold and silver coins.

They create small gold coins that weigh 1 ounce (oz.), 1/2 oz., 1/4 oz., 1/10 and 1/20 oz.

These coins were measured in **Troy ounces**, which means 12 ounces per pound rather than the standard 16 ounces.

The silver coins are of the same weight. However, it takes 15 silver coins to equal a gold coin of the same weight. So 15 silver coins weighing 1 oz. equals one gold coin weighing 1 oz.

15 silver coins = 1 gold coin.

Now the people on Gold Island can *price* all of their goods in terms of gold and silver coins (also known as *specie*).

The fisher does not need to make all those trades just to get baskets. The fisher can price the fish, and then trade the fish for gold or silver coins.

The basket weaver sets a price for baskets and accepts the gold and silver coins in trade.

The gold and silver coins become a "unit of account" that helps everyone easily relate the value of one item to another.

Anything of value that can be traded, both goods and services, now has a price in gold and silver coins.

And the economy of Gold Island speeds up.

Why?

Because money functions as a *medium of exchange*.

2. A medium of exchange

Obviously, the people of Gold Island can now exchange their goods and services much more easily.

- Money simplifies and speeds up trade.

- Money makes possible more division of labor.

- Money allows workers to price their skills more easily creating specialized skills.

Prices can change easily, even day by day.

If a product is suddenly in greater demand, the price can be raised.

If people think the price is too high and stop buying, the price can be dropped immediately.

The community becomes more effective and efficient. And the people's standard of living begins to rise more rapidly.

3. A store of value

Tor can pay his fishers gold and silver for the fish they catch rather than pay them in fish. The fishers can spend the money right away, or they can save and store it to use later.

When money and prices are stable, the stored money can buy as much later as it does the day it's stored. In other words, in a stable economy the money maintains its *purchasing power*, and then saving money can be encouraged.

Saved money can create capital.

As Tor builds his business, and his fishers and coconut gatherers continue working for him, he begins saving gold and silver coins.

This savings gives him flexibility. He can build his business by hiring more laborers, or he can build more fishing rods and slingshots to sell later.

These fishing rods and slingshots, otherwise known as durable goods, are called *capital assets*.

Capital creation can only happen out of stored savings.

A community or society with increasing capital can increase the quantity of goods.

Therefore, sound money, like gold and silver coins, results in an increasing standard of living for the community.

4. A unit of deferred payment

Money can be loaned to others when they have a strong need for it. The person who lends the money expects that the money repaid equals in value the money loaned, not counting interest.

In other words, the amount of goods and services the lender can buy now equals the amount the lender can buy later, once the borrower repays the loan.

If someone who has saved money discovers that the money will have less value over time, they will probably not save it. They would rather spend it now while it has more value.

When money loses purchasing power due to rising prices (popularly, but wrongly, called *inflation*), interest rates rise to compensate for the loss.

> One day, Alex comes to Tor and wants to borrow 20 gold coins to invest in a project. Tor thinks Alex has a good idea and decides to loan the 20 gold coins, but with *interest.*

> Tor expects Alex to pay him back 22 gold coins in six months.

Payment is therefore *deferred* for six months.

But the gold coins work only as units of deferred payment as long as the value of the coins is the same, six months later, as they are at the time he makes the loan.

If prices are rising steadily, then Tor will build into the rate of interest the amount of the rising prices.

In other words, if what 20 gold coins buy today will cost 21 gold coins in six months, Tor will add an additional gold coin to the amount to be paid back: a total of 23 gold coins.

Money that maintains its value as a unit of deferred payment helps keep interest rates low.

Low interest rates, and saved money that maintains its value, make long-term financing of projects possible.

Once again, sound money increases a community's standard of living.

A note on counterfeiting

Counterfeiting means that the value of the coin is not the same as the stated value stamped on the coin. In other words, if a gold coin is stamped with the words "1 oz. in Gold" but the coin weighs less than 1 oz., it is counterfeit.

*The stated value must be the same
as the actual value.*

Look at the gold coins below and notice the little mill marks on the edge. (Or look at your dimes, quarters, or half dollars.) Those marks have been milled onto the edge of the coins to keep people from *shaving* the coins.

Imagine the coins did not have these marks.

Bandits from Iron Island could take a bunch of coins and shave just a little bit of gold off of each one. Then they could melt down the gold and make another coin.

They could pass off the shaved coins, which have less gold in them, as if they held the full intrinsic value. They would have made counterfeit coins.

Gold and silver coins all have these mill marks to prevent shaving. Coins made out of nickel or copper (or zinc) do not have these marks because those coins are made of base metals, which hold much less value.

No one takes the time to shave base metals like pennies or nickels.

You may remember seeing old coins from Roman Empire that have a hole punched in the middle of them. When one of the corrupt Caesars, like Caligula, had too many parties and his treasury was nearly empty, he would order that holes be punched through gold and silver coins.

The corrupt Caesar would have the punched-out gold and silver melted down, coined, and then spent for more parties.

Then Caesar would order citizens to trade the punched coins as if they still held the full value. He would declare the counterfeit coins legitimate.

Of course, prices then would mysteriously begin to rise to make up for the reduced value in the coins. And workers would demand higher wages for the same work.

And then the government would institute wage and price controls to restrain the *greedy* business owners, and then...

But that's a story for another book.

Now you may be thinking...

What about the dimes and quarters and so-called silver dollars in my pocket right now that are all made out of the base metals of nickel, copper, and zinc?

They have mill marks.

But why should they, since they no longer contain gold or silver? Could someone be trying to make us think the value is the same? That the coins declared legitimate? Like Caesar declared his counterfeit coins to be?

And what about the paper euros and paper dollars and paper yen that I have in my purse or wallet right now?

That's money, right?

Well, it used to be...

Deep Dive: Government's Economic Role

If you believe that government should be a major player in influencing a country's economy, then you are likely a believer in government experts knowing better than the average person what is good for them.

Think about how elitist this idea is: People are fallible. People are not experts. People don't know what's good for them. People must be led by experts who know better.

But oddly, when people get government jobs, they seem to know better.

How is that idea working out? Especially once you recall that these "experts" are also fallible people, people subject like everyone else to vanity, greed, lust, anger, and other vices.

Government expertise fails to take into account the history of how power corrupts.

An example: If you take all the federal money allocated to helping the poor, you can calculate that it is over $200,000 per poor person each year.

Clearly, poor people are not getting all that money.

Who's getting it?

Many people like to say that government handouts create dependency. And that is true. For example, when a person in need manages to increase their income by $10,000 annually, they then lose over $15,000 in medical benefits.

What becomes the incentive to get a job?

The truth is that the dependency goes more the other way. Government is dependent on the poor. Why? Because it supports the livelihood of a lot of government workers.

Make no mistake—the *intentions* of these workers may be honorable. But they have no incentive to achieve the honorable goal of eliminating poverty.

This fact explains why the Great Society programs that started in the 1960s to help the poor have actually had the unintended consequence of increasing poverty.

Thomas Sowell tells the story of his experience of being a committed Marxist who got a job with the Federal Bureau of Labor Statistics. A Marxist believes in socialism, a socioeconomic system based on social ownership of the means of production, distribution based on one's contribution and production organized directly for use.

In layman's terms, *from each according to his ability, to each according to his needs.* In other words, the moral goal of equal distribution is set without regard for incentives.

Imagine that among a dozen workers, you work twice as many hours as the others, and some of the others are not working at all. Yet the fruits of your labor are equally distributed. At what point do you decide that working harder than others makes no sense?

Thomas Sowell wanted the job because he believed in statistics. He believed in getting the facts to prove that government economic intervention helped people. That socialism worked.

At that time, the government had mandated a federal minimum wage. Sowell had accumulated data, the facts, that demonstrated without ambiguity, that the federal minimum wage was hurting the people it was designed to help.

And nobody in the agency cared. Nobody was interested in changing the policy. Why? Because if government is seen to have an adverse economic effect with its programs, the result would be a lesser need for government. That is, fewer government workers.

Chapter 7

Paper Currency

The trifling economy of paper, as a cheaper medium, or its
convenience of transmission, weighs nothing in opposition to
the advantages of the precious metals; that it is liable to be
abused, has been, is, and forever will be abused, in every
country in which it is permitted.
Thomas Jefferson,
letter to John W. Eppes, Nov. 6, 1813

People don't like carrying heavy coins everywhere they go.

Today the word *currency* is used mainly to mean money. To avoid confusion, we will use the word money for coins (gold and silver) and currency for paper notes.

Let's talk about a new innovation that happens resulting from trade between the people of Gold Island and Silver Island.

> The people of Gold Island and Silver Island begin trading. Both have created the same system of money, using gold and silver coins of similar value.
>
> The main difference is that Gold Island money is stamped with the words "Gold Island" and Silver Island money is stamped with the words "Silver Island."
>
> Iron Island bandits don't care about trade and coins, except for those that they can steal.
>
> Both Gold Island and Silver Island accept the other island's money because the weight is the same for the same kind of coin.
>
> Both islands benefit from trade. The people of Gold Island make the best fishing poles and slingshots. They have skill sets that the people of Silver Island don't have.
>
> The people of Silver Island also create all kinds of different tools, silks, crafts, and other goods that the people of Gold Island can't produce.

Since both economies have grown strong, a lot of gold and silver coins get used. Some people are getting very rich. And gold and silver coins are heavy to carry.

So one of the good persons on Silver Island comes up with a new idea.

Why not become a goldsmith?

A goldsmith is someone who stores gold for travelers and merchants and charges a small storage fee.

The idea catches on and someone on Gold Island starts a goldsmithing business as well. Goldsmiths store gold and silver coins, have hired security to prevent the Iron Island bandits from stealing it, and charge people a small storage fee.

In place of the coins, the goldsmith gives the traveler or merchant an official slip of paper that reads something like this:

"Tor has on deposit with the Silver Island Goldsmith 20 ounces in gold and 65 ounces in silver. Payable on demand."

Each note is signed both by the goldsmith and by the traveler. The goldsmith keeps a record of all transactions.

The paper is an IOU note for the gold and silver coins that are stored.

The traveler can now go to market and wander around town without carrying all that weight in coins.

And the traveler does not have to worry that a bandit from Iron Island (or one of the less honest people from Silver Island) will rob him or her of those coins.

After a while, the goldsmith on Gold Island has an idea. Each paper IOU note is specifically created for each person.

What if the IOU notes had a more general design that is not specific to the person?

The IOU note might read something like this:

"Will pay to the bearer 20 ounces in gold, payable on demand at the Silver Island Goldsmith."

What if the goldsmith created different values for different notes?

There would be a whole set of IOU notes. And the people could trade IOU notes with each other.

In other words, the traveler can get a set of IOUs from the goldsmith:

Four notes would be for 5 ounces in gold, three notes would be for 10 ounces in silver, five notes would be for 5 ounces in silver, and ten notes would be for 1 ounce in silver.

The traveler can go to local merchants and trade the paper notes for goods and services. The merchants know that they can always go to the goldsmith and receive the gold and silver coins.

The goldsmith charges a small fee for each storage transaction. And everyone is happy.

Now here is where everyone's understanding of money begins to break down. Pay close attention:

The paper notes are not money.

Paper notes are IOUs.

Paper notes are symbols of money.

Paper notes are NOT money.

We will be exploring what less-than-honest people on Silver Island can do with paper notes in the chapter on _Inflation._

For now, let's see what other good things can come from the honest people on Gold Island.

Deep Dive: The Founder's Economics

When George Washington, James Madison, Alexander Hamilton, and many others convened the Constitutional Convention in Philadelphia in 1787. One of their major goals was to correct the deficits of the Articles of Confederation and put the federal government on a sound financial footing.

They knew from direct experience what economic havoc speculators could wreck, especially when paper currency was involved.

You may have heard of the phrase, *Not worth a continental?* They know what could happen to currency not backed by real money.

So in the U.S. Constitution, they ensured that the new federal government would close the door to such economic havoc. They did it in two ways.

1) In Article I. Section 8, they wrote, "The Congress shall have Power... To coin Money, regulate the Value thereof....

2) Section. 10. No State shall... make any Thing but gold and silver Coin a Tender in Payment of Debts....

Look more closely at Section 8. Notice that the founders said the Congress shall have the power to *coin* money, not to *print* money. They did not want Congress to have the power to print paper money.

Some would argue, Wait. Sure, they wanted Congress to make coins, but that doesn't mean they were closing the door to paper money.

Yes, it does. Remember, the purpose of the U.S. Constitution is to *define explicitly* the power of the new federal government. That government could not exercise any power not clearly defined.

If there were any doubt, Section 10 should clear it. In that section, Congress said that no state shall make anything but gold and silver legal tender in payment of debts. In other words, states could not make paper currency a legal tender as well. All taxes must be paid in gold or silver.

And the curious thing is, these two articles regarding money have never been amended. They are still the law of the land.

So how did Congress get around those constitutional provisions?

Chapters 9 and 10 on Inflation and A History of U.S. Money will give you a glimmer of what maneuvers were needed to circumvent the law of the land.

MONEY AND WEALTH

Chapter 8

Banking

"...banking establishments are more dangerous than standing armies..."
Thomas Jefferson,
letter to John Taylor, May 28, 1816

Thomas Jefferson obviously makes a strong statement about banking.

In later chapters, we will see the nature of his concern. For now, let's talk about what can be *good* about banks run by people with a moral conscience and who believe in free choice.

When real money is saved, when *wealth* is saved, it can be used to do good work.

How?

By making money available for *capital investments.*

> The goldsmith on Gold Island has a thriving business. Everyone trusts him. He stores people's gold and silver, charges a reasonable fee for the service, and protects their money.
>
> They have found the paper notes convenient to use for trade, and they can get their money from the goldsmith any time they want.
>
> Time passes, and the goldsmith notices something. No matter how many transactions he has every day, the amount of gold and silver never falls below the equivalent of 100,000 ounces in gold.
>
> The goldsmith has an idea. He could *loan* some of that gold to Tor, who wants to expand his fishing rod business.
>
> Tor has all kinds of ideas about how to make fishing rods, nets, lures, and all other fishing equipment in faster and more efficient ways. He just needs some money.

So the goldsmith and Tor talk with some of the depositors who use the goldsmith's service. They have an idea that will make everyone money.

Tor will borrow 10,000 oz. of gold for six months. He will pay it back with an *interest rate* of 1%. In other words, he will pay back 10,100 oz. of gold for the privilege of borrowing the gold.

Two depositors agree to allow the goldsmith to loan 5,000 oz. of gold from each of them. In return, each depositor will get 45 oz. of gold (a total 90 oz.), and the goldsmith will get 10 oz. of gold for making the arrangements.

Everyone understands they are taking a risk. Tor's idea may not work. Something may happen that will make it impossible for him to pay back the gold.

But everyone thinks the risk is worth it.

Tor borrows the money, hires workers (creates jobs), creates new products (creates wealth in the form of *capital* goods), and his business takes off. After six months he is already making more than 100 gold oz. each month.

Tor easily pays back the loan, plus interest. Everyone makes money by making the saved money do extra work. The risk paid off.

Now the goldsmith has become a banker.

Honest bankers provide a service that makes money for everyone: depositors, borrowers, and bankers.

By using the saved money to make capital investments in people with good ideas, bankers and depositors create more wealth, not only for individual borrowers and depositors, but also for the community.

> More and more people on Gold Island see the value of allowing the banker to lend their money and receiving part of the interest made on that money.
>
> Soon even the local council sees an opportunity. People still travel the island by walking or using horses. But the paths traveled are bumpy and sometimes rough.
>
> The local council has an idea and offers it to the community of taxpayers: If taxpayers are willing to pay the costs, the local council will borrow 20,000 oz. of gold to build some roads.
>
> Some people in the community will have short-term jobs, and everyone will benefit from the roads. After six months, the local council will collect enough taxes to pay back to the banker 20,200 oz. in gold.
>
> The tax could come in the form of tolls on people who use the roads. This then is an example of a good tax. The tax is a

consumption tax, because only the people who use the roads pay the tax.

Yes, it is a risk. There could be a storm that wipes out materials and work partially done. But the local council chooses a time of year when the weather is not much of a problem.

The banker, depositors, and taxpayers agree.

They get new roads.

The banker and depositors make money.

Everyone is happy with a much higher standard of living for the community.

Life is good when people have the choice to save money, take thoughtful risks, and put wealth to work creating more wealth, thus raising the standard of living for everyone.

So what can possibly go wrong?

Deep Dive: Understanding Prices

The Wonder of markets is that they reconcile the choices of myriad individuals.
William Easterly,
The White Man's Burden: Why the West's Efforts to Aid the Rest Have Done So Much Ill and So Little Good

People like to call the free market system a *profit* system. In fact, it is a *profit-and-loss* system.

Profits tell producers that people want more of something. Losses tell producers that people don't want more of something. Therefore, losses force producers to stop producing.

This is another reason why governments can distort markets. Governments routinely *force* people to buy products and services they don't want.

A market economy is so complex and varied that no expert can ever hope to get a handle on the true needs and desires of the millions of people engaged in markets. This is the wonder of prices.

Prices determine how much of a scarce resource gets used where, and how products get transferred to all those people. But prices are not just about transferring money. Prices provide financial incentives to affect behavior in the use of those scarce resources. They guide both consumers and producers, thus creating an effective and efficient *profit-and-loss* economic system.

As demand rises for a particular product, prices increase, signally the need for producers to produce more. As demand decreases, supply also decreases. In a free market economy, supply and demand affect production levels and pricing.

Remember, only when some instrument of force is introduced (or some natural limitation in nature) do we get constraints on production that keep prices artificially high. Although this can happen with corrupt businesses, it more often happens with corrupt or well-meaning government.

Chapter 9

Inflation

All the perplexities, confusion and distress in America arise,
not from the defects in their constitution or confederation,
not from want of honor or virtue, so much as from
downright ignorance of the nature of coin, credit, and
circulation.
John Adams,
letter to Thomas Jefferson, August 28, 1787

When everyone is honest, bankers, government workers,
wealth creators, and taxpayers all benefit.

But what happens when people are less than honest?

Let's follow the thinking of the goldsmith on Silver Island, who sees things just a little different from the goldsmith on Gold Island.

> Like the goldsmith on Gold Island, the goldsmith on Silver Island creates paper notes (IOUs) to represent the actual money (gold and silver) that people deposit with him.
>
> The amount of the notes exactly equals the amount of gold and silver coins he has on deposit. If there are 100,000 oz. of gold and silver on deposit, there are notes equaling 100,000 oz. of gold and silver in circulation.
>
> How much money is there in total?

> *If you answered 200,000...*
> *No! No! No!*
> *The total is still only 100,000 in money.*

> Only the gold and silver coins on deposit are money. The paper notes are *symbols* of that money.

> *Paper notes are NOT money.*
> *They are currency.*

> But the goldsmith on Silver Island notices that almost everyone who uses the paper notes *thinks of them* as money. Some people almost never come to redeem their notes for actual money.

They are happy to use the paper notes for trade and payment.

Workers begin asking employers to pay them in paper notes rather than gold and silver coins. The workers know they can trade them in at any time, but why bother?

Paper notes are so much more convenient to carry.

The Silver Island goldsmith then has a crafty idea.

> *What if he printed up extra notes?*
> *And spent them?*
> *Who would notice?*

You can see how tempting it would be to the goldsmith who is normally honest, but who suddenly has a medical expense.

Remember, this is Silver Island. The people here are a mix of good and bad. Sometimes they know it, and sometimes they don't.

On Silver Island, some otherwise good people can rationalize something bad as being good.

The goldsmith's child needs help and he is short on money.

Why not just "borrow the money" now by printing up a few extra paper notes to pay the doctor?

Then just pay it back later by destroying the other paper notes when he collects his storage fees?

No one would know. And besides, it's good for the child.

So the goldsmith does print up the extra notes. And nobody notices. And the child gets better. And the goldsmith pays back the "money."

What he does is a good thing, right?

As time goes by, the goldsmith rationalizes other bad actions as being good.

Why not print extra paper notes to buy better food, pay someone to rebuild the fence, and get his wife a nice gift?

He figures that since nobody notices, why should he even pay it back?

He works hard for a living. So what if he has a few extra nice things. Nobody notices. Nobody cares.

Soon for every 100 oz. of gold stored, there are notes circulating for 110 oz. of gold.

*And prices around town
begin to mysteriously rise.*

What the goldsmith on Silver Island does not realize, and almost everyone else as well, is this:

When more paper notes are "spent" and put into circulation, merchants notice that more goods are in demand.

When demand rises, the value of what people buy rises, and therefore merchants naturally charge more.

More paper notes = Rising demand = Rising prices

Supply and demand. Cause and effect. Choice being exercised in a free society.

A year later, the goldsmith on Silver Island decides to support another islander for election to the local council.

Together they hatch a scheme to outspend their opponent. The goldsmith prints up a lot of extra paper notes and donates it to the candidate's campaign.

Because, you know, his opponent has bad ideas, so the extra paper notes are really a good thing, you know, for the good of everybody.

More notes begin to circulate as the candidate spends the extra notes for political influence.

And prices mysteriously rise.

The candidate is elected and begins putting pressure on the goldsmith. Print up more notes so that the government can hire extra people. And spend money on community projects.

The goldsmith does.

And prices mysteriously continue to rise.

Who is to blame for the higher cost of living?

The politician blames the greedy merchants. And the merchants don't know what to say. They do not understand the real cause of the rising prices.

But the merchants, and actual creators of wealth, continue to be called greedy and uncaring.

They do not realize that the rising prices are a natural result of the *inflation.*

What is meant by inflation?

You know what happens when you inflate a balloon. As more air is pushed into the balloon, the amount of air increases.

What increases when you have economic inflation?

The supply of paper notes (currency).

Government, and people who make a living off of debt, will tell you that inflation is rising prices, just a natural force of nature, without anyone causing it.

Right?

Wrong!

Inflation is NOT rising prices.
Inflation CAUSES prices to rise.

As the currency supply increases, prices are forced to rise.

If you think the definition of something makes no difference, then you are a good target for con artists.

What if I can plant the idea in your mind that inflation is merely the rising of prices?

I can keep you from seeing the cause-and-effect relationship between printing paper notes and rising prices.

And if I can plant the idea in your mind that government debt is a *good* idea, then government can continue creating money out of thin air.

To do what?

To finance projects, wars, entitlements, and many other government "goods."

Who pays?

Workers who create wealth and become taxpayers are the ones who pay. Not the ones whose income is paid out of tax money.

The bankers and politicians on Silver Island soon tell the public that they have to withdraw gold and silver from circulation.

Why?

Because there's not enough to go around, and besides, the paper notes work well as money.

And almost everyone believes them, except a few kooks who talk about some kind of conspiracy between bankers and politicians.

But nobody really believes them.

Let's look at how governments change the definitions of money in order to take wealth away from you without you realizing they are doing it:

Through currency inflation and changing definitions.

Chapter 10

A History of U.S. Money

That paper money has some advantages is admitted. But that its abuses also are inevitable, and, by breaking up the measure of value, makes a lottery of all private property, cannot be denied. Shall we ever be able to put a constitutional veto on it?
Thomas Jefferson,
letter to Dr. Josephus B. Stuart, May 10, 1817

As you read this chapter, please:

Don't freak out!

Ripping away the pretty mask of government financial actions often causes people to act rashly: protesting taxes, going on anti-government campaigns, making emotional investments.

The history of U.S. money reflects practices
that governments have engaged in
for thousands of years.

All governments today have done what the U.S. government has done.

You've heard that power corrupts, and absolute power corrupts absolutely. Manipulating the definitions of money is standard practice for power brokers, both in government and in financial institutions.

I propose that, by going through this history, you will be better informed to make financial decisions. If you freak out instead, you take on unnecessary risks.

Okay. Let's begin...

Here is an example of legitimate paper money, a U.S. Gold Certificate, issued 1863-1934. Pay attention to its exact legal language:

THIS CERTIFIES THAT THERE HAVE
BEEN DEPOSITED IN THE TREASURY OF

THE UNITED STATES OF AMERICA

TEN DOLLARS

IN GOLD PAYABLE TO THE BEARER ON
DEMAND

Notice that on the left between the words "Gold" and "Certificate" is the statement: "This certificate is a legal tender in the amount thereof in payment of all debts and dues public and private."

This note is an IOU, just like those issued by the goldsmith on Gold Island.

It is not money.

It is a symbolic representation of real money, gold, on deposit in the U.S. treasury.

The bearer of this note can, ON DEMAND, trade it in for gold.

The same is true of Silver Certificates, issued 1886-1963.

THIS CERTIFIES THAT THERE HAVE BEEN DEPOSITED IN THE TREASURY OF

THE UNITED STATES OF AMERICA

ONE DOLLAR

IN SILVER PAYABLE TO THE BEARER ON DEMAND

Notice how the language has been simplified to the left of the president:

THIS CERTIFICATE IS LEGAL TENDER
FOR ALL DEBTS PUBLIC AND PRIVATE

One thing should be obvious about both of these certificates: Neither is gold or silver.

But a couple of things are not so obvious:

Notice that the gold certificate will pay ten *dollars in gold*. And the silver certificate will pay *one dollar in silver*. These certificates are *not* dollars.

Remember from previous chapters when we talked about measuring gold in ounces. Well gold and silver were also measured in *dollars*.

Think about it this way: Suppose someone came up to you and said, "Do you want to buy a gallon?"

You would be confused.

Why?

Because that question makes no sense.

You would rightly ask, "A gallon of what? A gallon of milk? A gallon of gas?"

> *A unit of measurement has no meaning*
> *except when it measures something.*

Notice that the gold and certificates measure something: ten dollars in gold coin, one dollar in silver.

In earlier days, if one person asked another, "Would you like a dollar?" the person asked would answer, "A dollar of what? Gold? Silver?"

Definitions of words are important. When you change the definition, you change the picture people hold in their minds.

> *Therefore, manipulating definitions*
> *is one method of a kind of mind control.*

In 1913 the U.S. Congress passed the Federal Reserve Act. Soon after, the Federal Reserve began issuing Federal Reserve Notes (FRN).

And the language began a subtle transformation. The first FRNs stated that they were redeemable in gold on demand (see the text to the left of the president).

But do you notice a subtle change in the language of the note?

First, in the text to the left, there is a new phrase. The note is redeemable "in gold or *lawful money* at any Federal Reserve Bank."

So the Federal Reserve can have something *other than* gold as lawful money?

Perhaps they mean silver, or something else. But there is another subtle shift in the language.

Can you see it?

Look at the text above and below the president.

FEDERAL RESERVE NOTE

WILL PAY TO THE BEARER ON DEMAND

FIVE DOLLARS

See the shift? Even though the note elsewhere states the note is redeemable in gold or lawful money, the note now states the unit of measurement (five dollars) disconnected from gold or lawful money.

Isn't that interesting?

The Federal Reserve issued the FRN pictured above in 1928. Six years later it issued the FRN pictured below.

See something missing?

The statement to the left of the president says, "This note is legal tender for all debts public and private and is redeemable in lawful money at the United States Treasury or at any Federal Reserve Bank."

The note has been completely disconnected from gold.

You may recall that President Franklin Delano Roosevelt made the ownership of gold illegal and withdrew it from circulation. (Much like the bankers and politicians on Silver Island.)

Now people were expected to redeem these notes for silver or whatever the government deemed as lawful money.

Not a problem, right?

Let's see...

In 1963 the Federal Reserve Bank took the next step in transforming (redefining) U.S. money. They began withdrawing silver from the economy that year. They also issued a new FRN.

To the left of the president is the statement, "This note is legal tender for all debts public and private."

Above and below the president was this text:

FEDERAL RESERVE NOTE

THE UNITED STATES OF AMERICA

ONE DOLLAR

Notice anything missing?

No mention of gold, silver, lawful money, or anything making this note redeemable. Before 1963 all U.S. paper money measured gold, silver, and lawful money in *dollars*— a dollar in gold, a dollar in silver, a dollar in lawful money.

But in 1963 that all changed.

Citizens and foreign governments were expected to forget redeeming notes. Instead the note proclaims itself as one or more dollars.

In 1963 when the first FRNs were issued about the time of President Kennedy's assassination, a mother could go into a bank with a pile of silver dollars and deposit them. Then, remembering, turn around and say, placing a FRN on the counter, "I forgot. It's my daughter's birthday, and I want to give her a silver dollar."

And the bank teller would respond, "We're sorry, but all silver dollars are being withdrawn and replaced with FRNs, because, you know, there is just not enough silver to go around, and it makes more economic sense to transition to a paper money, which are just as good as any dollar, you see."

All the new coins were made, not with silver, but with nickel and copper.

By 1971, the U.S. government had printed up so much "money" that France and other countries began to distrust its value. They began trading in U.S. "dollars" for gold in the U.S. Treasury. To stop this run on gold, President Nixon ended the "Gold Standard."

This action simply meant that FRNs were no longer redeemable. The government keeps the gold and silver, and everyone else gets paper.

That's a fair exchange for a working economy, right?

Today's currency is not money.
It has no intrinsic value.

And as the government via the Federal Reserve prints up more money (electronically these days), the value of that money decreases. But real gold and silver preserves value.

In 1971, gold was valued at $35 per ounce. As of this writing (summer 2013) gold is valued at $1,400 per ounce.

In the early 1960s, a gallon of gas could be purchased in some areas of the country for a silver quarter. Today that silver quarter can still buy you a gallon of gas in many areas of the country.

Gold and silver tend to preserve their value. Even though more *dollars* are needed to buy an ounce of gold, that ounce of gold or silver still buys the same *value* of things it used to buy.

In sum, governments that control money and currency will find ways to spend what they don't have. Since citizens do not generally understand the nature of coin, currency, and circulation, nor do they like ever rising taxes, governments find ways of indirectly taxing them through inflation.

Money can't be created out of thin air, but currency can. And the result of more paper chasing goods and services is a rise in the cost of goods and services.

We've discussed money and banking and inflation and currency. Next up: credit and debt.

Are there any traps in how we think about credit and debt?

You bet there is.

Side Notes

Note 1

By the way, have you ever wondered who got all the gold and silver that was withdrawn from circulation?

Note 2

Remember the "mill marks" that were engraved on the edges of coins to stop people from shaving the coins and melting down the shavings?

Gold and silver coins had those mill marks, but nickel and copper coins did not. No one shaves base metal coins and melts down the shavings for their value.

But now that dimes, quarters, half-dollars, and dollars are made of nickel and copper, why keep the mill marks?

Perhaps to keep up the illusion that they are money?

Deep Dive: Minimum Wage Laws

Supply-and-demand says that above-market prices create unsaleable surpluses, but that has not stopped most of Europe from regulating labor markets into decades of depression-level unemployment.
Bryan Caplan,
The Myth of the Rational Voter:
Why Democracies Choose Bad Policies

The prime example of how a government with good intentions can distort an economy and harm the people it intends to help is minimum wage laws.

If you have understood all that has been discussed so far, you can likely predict what happens when employers are forced to pay employees more, due to an artificial law that makes it illegal to pay less than a certain amount.

A basic economic fact is this: Prices artificially raised tend to cause more to be supplied and less demanded.

In other words, if the price of labor (workers now needing to be paid a higher minimum wage) goes up, then an employer can only afford to hire fewer workers. And employers will tend to look for those workers with greater skills, who embody a greater value for what they are being paid.

In other words, lesser-skilled workers, those the minimum wage is usually designed to help, end up with fewer jobs available for them to accept.

Demand for those workers goes down.

The data has long been presented to support this common economic fact. But few with good intentions seem to respond to the data. Instead, they talk about the greed of employers and businesses.

Greed there may be, though not in every case. But greed or a non-artificial increase in prices cause people real harm, people who are the targets of the well-intentioned.

Chapter 11

Credit and Debt

*"He that sells upon Credit, expects to lose 5 per Cent. by bad
Debts; therefore he charges, on all he sells upon Credit, an
Advance that shall make up that Deficiency."*
Benjamin Franklin
Poor Richard's Almanack, 1737

Credit offers you the opportunity to go into debt...

...And debt is slavery.

Why slavery?

When you owe money, you have to work to pay it off. You cannot live a life free from work. Nor are you free to work to make money that you are free to spend as you wish.

So credit and debt are two sides of the same coin.

For most people, credit comes in the form of credit cards. Let's look at the idea of credit cards more closely.

> On Silver Island, people trade goods and services using paper money. Two people can transact business without a third party being present.

> Zane, a farmer, needs tools, and trades paper money with Lori, a store owner, for those tools.

> However, Jon, a goldsmith and banker, observes them and thinks, "There has to be a way I can make money on their transactions."

> Jon has an idea.

> He creates a little card that says, "Jon's Credit Trust & Savings." He gets approval from the local council by explaining how it would be in everyone's interest to allow easy credit. Jon reminds them how much value the community got from aqueducts and other public projects that benefited everyone.

Why not let individuals borrow, with a small interest rate, so that they can have more flexibility in their lives?

Good idea, right?

So Jon offers his little card to people saying, "Hey, you don't have to have money to spend money. If you need something now, you can pay later, plus a small fee. And if you pay it off within a month, you don't have to pay a fee."

The idea catches on. Some people use the card and are smart enough to pay it off at the end of each month. Others see the fee as small and so they don't mind paying a little extra.

People are still transacting in the same way, but a little bit of each transaction starts filling Jon's pockets.

Over time, there is some fraud and abuse, and non-payments, requiring Jon to hire debt collectors. He has to raise the interest rate on the card to cover the difference.

But that's fair, right?

The costs are spread among everyone, so the increase is small.

All of this sounds good until you realize where it is all headed. Originally interest rates were about 3%-5%. But when banks and financial institutions get greedy and hand out cards to anyone and everyone, what happens?

Remember when you were in college and credit cards began showing up in your mail?

Easy credit, right? Even though you didn't have a job?

Some people didn't pay them off and got bad credit. But as we have learned...

TANSTAAFL
There Ain't No Such Thing
As A Free Lunch.
Someone always pays.

So now we have interest rates routinely over 20%. With other kinds of service fees as well.

Credit cards, especially those that offer minimum payments that barely cover the interest rates, are designed to enslave you.

How?

By stimulating your desire to get things now, rather than wait for when you have the money. Then by offering a minimum payment that covers the interest, the amount you owe remains nearly the same.

You are still on the hook for paying the interest without having paid hardly anything on the principal amount you owe.

People who extend you credit are less interested in you paying off the debt. They're more interested in keeping you in debt just enough so you can make the monthly payments.

Imagine you are the creditor. You have 100,000 people using your credit cards. Ideally, they have reached their credit card limit (their debt ceiling) and are making only the interest payments.

You have a steady and massive income while everyone else works hard just to pay the interest.

All because you have convinced them that credit (that is, debt) is a good thing.

And if someone has enough money to pay more, reducing the principal, then what do you do?

You offer to *raise their credit limit*, so they can spend more, get more in debt, and have a higher minimum payment.

Debt is slavery.
The whole point is to keep you paying.

That's why credit card companies are less interested in how much debt you have. They want to know if you can make the monthly payments on time. If you can, you are a good customer.

Remember how they taught you in school to save money, buying only when you have saved enough money?

They emphasized frugality and thrift?

No, you don't remember that?

Did you have to look up the definitions of frugality and thrift?

Frugality means being careful about spending money, or not using things thoughtlessly so that you don't have to spend needlessly.

Thrift is similar: being careful about money management, saving for a rainy day, and avoiding debt.

More likely, schools taught you simple things about opening a checking account and building credit. How important it is to pay on time. How to at least pay the minimum payment. How to protect your credit rating so you can get loans.

In other words, they taught you, not how to be free, but how to manage being enslaved to debt.

When you buy a home, you will find something even more extraordinary, something called APR, and lots of talk about monthly payments over 30 years.

When buying a home, how often do you see the payment schedule?

Suppose you buy a $300,000 home at 7% interest over 30 years. If you look closely, you will see that the first few years of payments are almost all interest and no principal.

This means that you are paying just the profit that goes to the lender, not significantly paying down the actual loan.

After a few years of paying, you will still owe over $290,000.

If you stay with their payment schedule, your $300,000 home will cost more than $1 million.

In other words, the lender gets all of their profit up front, with you still owing almost the full amount.

And what if you get talked into a variable interest rate or a low interest rate for the first three years that goes up the fourth year?

You find out quickly that lenders start working hard to get you to refinance. You have been set up to lower your monthly payments and start at $300,000 again.

Suppose you have made payments for decades and you owe less than $150,000. You now have *equity*.

When you have equity in your home, you have built up inherent value that you can use. Equity is the difference between the value and what you owe.

For example, if your home is valued at $300,000, and you owe only $100,000 on the mortgage, then your equity is around $200,000.

You could take out a *second mortgage* for as much as $200,000. Generally, such second mortgages are used to improve the home, or solve some immediate financial need.

Lenders regard an equity loan as safe because you have no choice but to pay it back one way or another.

In other words, if you cannot make the payments, they take your home.

Isn't that nice?

When it comes to home ownership, you should pay for the home outright, or you should rent it out for more than the payments.

Or if you want to live in it with a mortgage, be sure to have the money to pay down the principal in those first ten years.

Pay extra payments that apply

to the principal only.

You can knock several years off the mortgage and save tens or even hundreds of thousands of dollars in interest.

Remember, if you learn nothing else from this little book, learn this.

Debt is slavery.

Let's explore what can be done to invest thoughtfully in a world that loves debt.

Chapter 12

Investments

*Rule #3: Recognize the difference between
investing and speculating.*
Harry Browne, from *Fail-Safe Investing*

The key to being safe with your wealth is to *keep it simple.*

Unless you plan on being a financial and investment expert, you want your money and wealth to be safe.

Many people make the mistake of building their retirement primarily on investments. And many more mistake real investments with speculations.

Imagine going into a casino and playing the slot machine.

Is that an investment?

Of course not. You know very well that the odds are against you getting any return at all. You are taking a chance. You are *gambling*. There is no guarantee to win.

Casinos may want you to think that the odds get better the more you play. Isn't that what all the government-sponsored lotteries want you to believe?

Some casinos may even say that by playing more, you are *investing* your money and are more likely to win.

They are lying. Gambling is always speculation because there is always a chance of losing your money.

A bank that pays interest on money you save is doing something different. The bank does not take your money. The bank uses your money to make loans and pays you some of the interest they charge on the loan.

You can't lose your money, as long as the bank is in business.

Therefore, you are not speculating. You are investing.

But what happens when government inflates the currency supply, and the value of your currency goes down?

What happens when your savings in a bank gets an interest rate that turns out to be below the rate of inflation?

Is saving your money in a bank still an investment? Or has the government turned it into speculation?

What if someone says you should *invest* in the stock market?

Since you can lose any money you put in the stock market, the stock market is not an investment. It's a form of gambling. It's speculation.

> **An investment** *is safe and delivers a real return that you can predict.*

> **A speculation** *is unsafe and risks losing your money.*

These days, many people are realizing that putting trust in governments, in stocks, and in retirement programs may not be the best idea.

And often people are too willing to invest quickly in something that appears to be an easy money-maker, when in fact they are speculating on something that will cost them dearly.

These are called *economic bubbles.*

> You've probably heard about the first economic bubble, the Dutch Tulip Bulb craze in the 1630s.
>
> Tulip bulbs were first introduced in the Netherlands at that time. People craved them so much that the price of tulip bulbs rose quickly. At a certain point, people thought it a good idea to buy the bulbs to resell later for a higher price.
>
> The prices rose so quickly that buying them became a mania. At the peak, reports say that bulbs were sold for 10 times the annual salary of a skilled craftsman. Another report says that one bulb was sold for 12 acres of land.
>
> Soon the bubble burst, and many people lost their savings.

Buying now and selling higher later is the essence of speculation. Speculation is not the same as investment. And people who do not understand bubbles let themselves be carried away by crazy speculations. Those who do understand bubbles profit from them.

There are stock bubbles, high-tech bubbles, housing bubbles, and more. As of this writing (2013), the world is seeing both stock and housing bubbles. These bubbles are formed from a general credit bubble; so much bailout money is being created out of thin air, it has to go somewhere.

There's a consequence when governments print up money out of thin air to "stabilize" the economy; that money has to go somewhere, so it's used for speculation. Of course, when the bubbles burst, the economy will be anything but stable.

As we have seen with Silver Island, when the currency supply is inflated, governments and financial institutions can profit for a while.

When the government is increasing the money supply, suppress any impulse you have to speculate on stocks or real estate (the classic bubbles). You may find a way to properly invest in real estate (buy a home or property that you intend to develop, and thereby increase its value, its equity).

But avoid snap decisions for something that looks like a quick way to make money. Unless you are a financial whiz, you will be the one transferring money to financial whizzes.

Con Artist Investments

When you have money, you will find that many financial advisers will advise you to invest. They will say, "Your money needs to be put to work. Otherwise, you are wasting it."

In certain economies, their advice is good. But when governments go into massive debt, all bets are off. Sometimes, good advisers who do not know better, or through no fault of their own, begin giving bad advice. Others may simply be looking to profit off of investing your money.

There are some signs of a financial con artist. The main con takes the form of a *pyramid scheme.*

The classic pyramid scheme is the *chain letter.* Or *chain email.*

"Send $10 to the person who sent you this email. Then send this email to ten people you know and have them send you $10. Everyone will spend $10 and receive $100. It's a sure thing."

Is it?

Here are some tips:

1. Watch for anything that asks you to get more investors to join. If you are told that you profit when someone else invests, you may be part of a pyramid scheme.

The classic scheme is this: You buy into my plan for $10, and I will tell you my plan for you to make easy money. It can't fail. You give me $10, and then I tell you to get 5 other people to give you $10 for a plan. Part of the plan is that you give me only $1 of each $10. Then you tell them your plan to go out and get another 5 people to give them $10, and then pass on $1 to you.

When you do that, I make $15 from you. You make $50, minus the $10 you gave to me for the plan, and then the $5 you give me for the 5 people you enlisted. So you make $35.

For essentially doing nothing. You make something for nothing.

It can't fail, right?

Wrong. It always fails. People who do not understand exponential progressions get suckered into this pyramid scheme. It's a pyramid because there are a few people at or near the top (who make money), but the pyramid breaks down as you near the bottom.

Think of it this way. You have a chessboard with 64 squares. You put one penny on the first square. You put two on the second, four on the third, eight on the fourth, 16 on the fifth, and so on...

How much money do you put on the 64th square?

$184,467,440,737,095,516.15.

That's over 184 *trillion* dollars!

2. Some pyramid schemes label themselves as *multilevel marketing*. Many multilevel marketing businesses can be legitimate when they are based on an actual, valuable product or service.

But any system that requires you to make money *primarily* from getting new recruits is a risk. It's actually a pyramid scheme. Sooner or later you run out of new recruits.

3. Some government programs are pyramid schemes and are unsustainable.

If they promise that some people pay in to support people who never pay in, or have no accountability for the money they get, then eventually the number of people receiving will outnumber those paying. Then the scheme breaks down.

Protecting Yourself

So what to do?

Probably the best advice for financial amateurs deals with balancing your investments by diversifying. The danger arises when you invest all you have in one or a few investments.

Harry Browne has developed one such balanced investment program. (His is not the only one.) He wrote a simple book called *Fail-Safe Investing*.

The book contains The Simple 17 Rules of Financial Safety. I suggest you get his book to get schooled in all of these rules.

Here's a sample:

Rule #1: Build your wealth upon your career

Rule #5: Don't expect anyone to make you rich

Rule #9: Do only what you understand

Rule #10: Spread your risk

Rule #12: Speculate only with money you can afford to lose

Harry provides something he calls the Bulletproof Portfolio, designed to take you through almost any government or economic action. The Bulletproof portfolio is built on three requirements:

1. Safety

2. Stability

3. Simplicity

The Bulletproof Portfolio is designed to protect you through the four possible economic situations:

1. Prosperity

2. Inflation

3. Recession

4. Deflation

The simplest way to protect your assets, according to the Bulletproof Portfolio, is to divide them into four investments equally (25% in each):

1. Stocks

2. Bonds

3. Gold

4. Cash

When any of the four possible economic situations occur, this investment balance keeps you from losing everything.

There's a lot more we could explore, but Harry Browne is the best at it. Get his book and see for yourself.

By the way, I know you are looking at stocks and thinking, *Isn't that speculation?*

Yes, but in terms of the overall Bulletproof Portfolio, it becomes a kind of investment. How to invest in stocks, and how to speculate in stocks, are two different matters.

We will not explore those distinctions here. It's best to begin with something simple. And the Bulletproof Portfolio is simple.

If you want to explore economic topics further, review the Recommended Reading list, particularly Richard Maybury's *Whatever Happened to Penny Candy?*

Maybury has written a series of books on money and government that are well worth reading. You may not agree with everything he says (I don't), but he provides enough history to back up many of his claims. And his arguments are worth exploring and understanding.

Investing in Yourself and Your Community

What do you do when you do not have lots of tangible assets, like gold and silver?

> *One way of thinking about investing and wealth is: Invest in yourself.*

Build your skills. Make your own decisions. Save in a variety of ways.

Wealth is something that holds intrinsic value. And there are many ways you can make yourself more intrinsically valuable.

Remember from *Creating Your Life* the section on Locus of Control?

> *Are you the cause of your life?*
> *Or the effect?*

> *Do you depend upon yourself primarily?*
> *Or on others?*

> *Do you make your life happen?*
> *Or do you count on others to make it happen?*

In the end, other people can be counted on to be focused on making *their* lives happen, not yours.

Taking responsibility for your money, your wealth, your finances, your investments, your ability to create a life, is the best way to acquire more freedom.

And *freedom* is what this series of books is all about.

As you think about money and creating your life, remember the fundamental idea that you can be a wealth creator. You can learn and grow, and develop a number of skills.

You can try your hand at being an entrepreneur. You can create your own business, as well as create your own life.

You create your life. That even includes when you give up your life to others. Sure, life does not always work out the way you expect. You have made decisions in the past that come back to you, whether you recall them or not.

That's life.

But if you know enough about how other people take advantage of your economic life, you can take your life back. The key is to start now.

Be **accountable** for your thoughts, your actions, your decisions, your debts, your assets.

It's really a better way to live.

> *It doesn't matter what happens to you,*
> *what matters is how you respond.*

Real wealth comes from both being fairly self-sufficient and being part of a healthy community. Although we live in a Silver Island world, the people of Gold Island have something to teach us.

> *Build real skills,*
> *both general and specific.*

General skills sometimes appear to be useless skills, such as reading, writing, and mathematics.

You may think that studying literary works, writing an expository essay, learning new and complex words, and mastering algebra or complex math problems without a calculator, have little use.

But they all exercise mental faculties that come into play in your daily life. Often in ways you don't realize.

Skills such as algebra, trigonometry, and calculus strengthen your ability to perceive complex abstractions, to hold more in your head. You may work on a farm and suddenly see mathematically new ways to improve the effectiveness of how you harvest a field.

Or you may meet someone who pulls at your heart and happens to love math.

Specific skills like...

- fixing a fence and programming a computer

- cooking a good meal and taking care of a baby

- learning how to type 40 words per minute and creating a PowerPoint presentation

- sewing on a button and writing a resume

...all of these build your capabilities. And the more capabilities you have, the more value you have to offer.

Neither of my parents went to college. They had no plan to prepare me for college.

I started working at a McDonald's fast-food restaurant at the age of 16. I worked at an auto-wrecking yard at 18. I worked at a small 7-11 store at 19. I put myself through college managing that 7-11 store.

Along the way, I learned how to program a computer, write an essay, solve a differential equation, read Shakespeare, compose on a piano, type 40 words per minute, understand Plato and Aristotle, study Spanish, French, and Latin, and teach a college class.

I published my first magazine article in an Apple computer magazine.

Instead of a computer programming degree, I got a degree in English.

I later taught business writing at a business college. I had completed graduate work in forensic rhetoric (the language of lawyers), and the dean of a law school heard me lecture on writing. He offered me a chance to teach Legal Writing to paralegals. I did that for two years.

I consulted for the California Commission on Police Officers Standards and Training, and for Intel Corporation. I worked in Silicon Valley for start-up companies, teaching myself PowerPoint and video script writing.

I learned how to direct and edit corporate videos over the course of 10 years while consulting.

I helped a semiconductor company with process engineer training in problem solving. They offered me my first corporate job in Learning and Development.

I traveled abroad, learning how to develop engineers and managers in China, Japan,

Korea, Taiwan, Singapore, France, and Germany.

My company offered a development program for advanced university degrees. They paid most of the cost of my degree in Organization and Management Development.

I wasn't lucky. I was prepared. When the window of opportunity opened, I was ready to walk through it, even when I didn't quite know what I was doing.

Nobody starts out knowing everything. I had no idea where I would end up. But by building a variety of skills and taking advantage of opportunities, new doors opened.

You have a choice.

Do you see life as luck? Or something you create?

Do you go through life depending mainly on others? Or is your plan to rely mainly on yourself?

Do you simply take from life and allow others to take from you? Or do you invest yourself and give to your community?

If you choose to live on the debt side of life, you choose being dependent on others. If you choose the asset side of life, you choose giving to yourself and your community.

True freedom is choosing… and choosing wisely.

Choose investing in yourself and your community. Choose true wealth.

And give up slavery.

The "Money and Wealth" Checklist

I am indeed rich,
since my income is superior to my expense,
and my expense is equal to my wishes.
Edward Gibbon, 1776

Wealth, trade, and jobs

__ Invest in yourself by building your specific skills and knowledge.

__ Be and do more; the more you can be and do, the more you have to trade, and to give.

__ Understand that you may have to sacrifice and pay your dues.

__ Let go of the lottery mentality (life is luck); cultivate the action mentality (life is created).

Government, taxes, and inflation

__ Be wary of supporting government debt.

__ Discover the difference between constructive and destructive taxes.

__ Understand how the government creates and benefits from inflation, a hidden tax.

__ Beware of supporting political programs that increase debt and dependency.

__ Support political programs that build in real accountability.

__ Don't respond radically when you understand how governments operate; know them, and plan your finances accordingly.

Money, currency, and banking

__ Educate yourself on the differences between wealth and money.

__ Own real money: gold and silver coins.

__ When dealing with precious metals, deal with reputable businesses (for example, beware of eBay, or people who make extravagant claims); but be watchful, even of reputable brokers.

Debt, credit, and investments

__ Avoid debt where possible; live a life where your assets are greater than your debts.

__ When you use credit cards, pay off the total amount each month.

__ Save a part of every paycheck.

__ Buy when you have the money; learn the value of delayed gratification.

__ Avoid paying interest; have people pay *you* interest.

__ Practice the virtues of thrift and frugality.

__ Be wary of get-rich-quick schemes; they are almost always a con.

__ Understand Harry Browne's Bulletproof Portfolio.

__ Invest in yourself, in building your own skills so you can take advantage of opportunities.

__ Find ways to support your community.

__ Give up being a slave.

* * *

The strongest bond of human sympathy, outside of the family relation, should be one uniting all working people, of all nations, and tongues, and kindreds. Nor should this lead to a war upon property, or the owners of property. Property is the fruit of labor—property is desirable—is a positive good in the world. That some should be rich, shows that others may become rich, and hence is just encouragement to industry and enterprise. Let not him who is houseless pull down the house of another; but let him labor diligently and build one for himself, thus by example assuring that his own shall be safe from violence when built.

Abraham Lincoln, reply to New York Workingmen's Democratic Republican Association March 21, 1864.

Recommended Reading

Browne, Harry. (1999.) *Fail-Safe Investing: Lifelong Financial Security in 30 Minutes.* New York: St. Martin's Press.

Friedman, Milton, and Friedman, Rose. (1979, 1990.) *Free to Choose: A Personal Statement.* Boston: Mariner Books.

Hazlitt, Henry. (1946, 1988.) *Economics in One Lesson: The Shortest and Surest Way to Understand Basic Economics.* New York: Three Rivers Press.

Maybury, Richard J. (2010.) *Whatever Happened to Penny Candy?.* Placerville, CA: Bluestocking Press.

Sowell, Thomas. (2015.) *Basic Economics: A Common Sense Guide to the Economy.* New York: Basic Books.

Sowell, Thomas. (2008.) *Economic Facts and Fallacies.* New York: Basic Books.

* * *

People are often reproached for wishing for money above all things and for loving it more than anything else; but it is natural and even inevitable for people to love that which, like an unwearied Proteus, is always ready to turn itself into whatever object their wandering wishes or manifold desires may for the moment fix upon.

Everything else can satisfy only one wish, one need: food is good only if you are hungry; wine, if you are able to enjoy it; drugs, if you are sick; fur for the winter; love for youth, and so on. These are all only relatively good. Money alone is absolutely good, because it is not only a concrete satisfaction of one need in particular; it is an abstract satisfaction of all.

Arthur Schopenhauer, from **The Wisdom of Life** (1897)

Appendix: Excerpts from Original Works

[edited without ellipses by Mark Andre Alexander]

Henry Hazlitt, from *Economics in One Lesson*

The bad economist sees only
what immediately strikes the eye;
the good economist also looks beyond.

The bad economist sees only
the direct consequences of the proposed course;
the good economist looks also
at the longer and indirect consequences.

The bad economist sees only
what the effect of a given policy has been
or will be on one particular group;
the good economist inquires also
what the effect of the policy will be on all groups.

⁕

Thomas Jefferson (1743-1826), from a letter to Dr. Josephus B. Stuart (May 10, 1817)

In copying [England] we do not seem to consider that like premises induce like consequences. The bank mania is one of the most threatening of these imitations. It is raising up a moneyed aristocracy in our country which has already set the government at defiance.

These have taken deep root in the hearts of that class from which our legislators are drawn. Their principles lay hold of the good, their [money gained dishonestly] of the bad, and thus those whom the Constitution had placed as guards to its portals, are sophisticated or suborned from their duties.

That **paper money** has some advantages, is admitted. But that its abuses also are inevitable, and, by breaking up the measure of value, makes a lottery of all private property, cannot be denied. Shall we ever be able to put a constitutional veto on it?

⁕

James Madison (1751-1836), from *The Federalist Papers #44* (1788)

The extension of the prohibition to bills of credit must give pleasure to every citizen, in proportion to his love of justice and his knowledge of the true springs of public prosperity.

The loss which America has sustained since the peace, from the pestilent effects of **paper money** on the necessary confidence between man and man, on the necessary confidence in the public councils, on the industry and morals of the people, and on the character of republican government, constitutes an enormous debt against the States chargeable with this unadvised measure, which must long remain unsatisfied; or rather an accumulation of guilt, which can be expiated no otherwise than by a voluntary sacrifice on the altar of justice, of the power which has been the instrument of it.

Jack Weatherford, from "Prometheus Unbound" in Lapham's Quarterly: About Money, Vol. I, No. 2, Spring 2008

Money took away power from priests and armies; it had the transformative ability to turn gold into democracy...Compared with the physical force of the military and the spiritual authority of religion, money offered a third and completely novel way to organize society. Without regard to rank, class, or standing, anyone with the proper coin could buy a goat or a turnip, a jug of wine or a basket of fish, a parcel of land for a vineyard or a pinch of salt to flavor dinner.

John Maynard Keynes (1883-1946), from Chapter VI of *Economic Consequences of the Peace* (1919)

Lenin is said to have declared that the best way to destroy the Capitalist System was to debauch the currency. By a continuing process of inflation, governments can confiscate, secretly and unobserved, an important part of the wealth of their citizens.

By this method they not only confiscate, but they confiscate *arbitrarily;* and, while the process impoverishes many, it actually enriches some. The sight of this arbitrary rearrangement of riches strikes not only at security, but at confidence in the equity of the existing distribution of wealth.

Those to whom the system brings windfalls, beyond their deserts and even beyond their expectations or desires, become "profiteers," who are the object of the hatred of the bourgeoisie, whom the inflationism has impoverished, not less than of the proletariat. As the inflation proceeds and the real value of the currency fluctuates wildly from month to month, all permanent relations between debtors and creditors, which form the ultimate foundation of capitalism, become so utterly disordered as to be almost meaningless; and the process of wealth-getting degenerates into a gamble and a lottery.

Lenin was certainly right. There is no subtler, no surer means of overturning the existing basis of society than to debauch the currency. The process engages all the hidden forces of economic law on the side of destruction, and does it in a manner which not one man in a million is able to diagnose.

In the latter stages of the war all the belligerent governments practiced, from necessity or incompetence, what a Bolshevist might have done from design. Even now, when the war is over, most of them continue out of weakness the same malpractices.

But further, the Governments of Europe, being many of them at this moment reckless in their methods as well as weak, seek to direct on to a class known as "profiteers" the popular indignation against the more obvious consequences of their vicious methods. These "profiteers" are, broadly speaking, the entrepreneur class of capitalists, that is to say, the active and constructive element in the whole capitalist society, who in a period of rapidly rising prices cannot help but get rich quick whether they wish it or desire it or not.

If prices are continually rising, every trader who has purchased for stock or owns property and plant inevitably makes profits. By directing hatred against this class, therefore, the European Governments are carrying a step further the fatal process which the subtle mind of Lenin had consciously conceived.

The profiteers are a consequence and not a cause of rising prices. By combining a popular hatred of the class of entrepreneurs with the blow already given to social security by the violent and arbitrary disturbance of contract and of the established equilibrium of wealth which is the inevitable result of inflation, these Governments are fast rendering impossible a continuance of the social and economic order of the nineteenth century.

But they have no plan for replacing it.

A sentiment of trust in the legal money of the State is so deeply implanted in the citizens of all countries that they cannot but believe that some day this money must recover a part at least of its former value. To their minds it appears that value is inherent in money as such, and they do not apprehend that the real wealth, which this money might have stood for, has been dissipated once and for all.

If a man is compelled to exchange the fruits of his labors for paper which, as experience soon teaches him, he cannot use to purchase what he requires at a price comparable to that which he has received for his own products, he will keep his produce for himself, dispose of it to his friends and neighbors as a favor, or relax his efforts in producing it.

⁂ ✳ ⁂

Frederic Bastiat (1801-1850),
from That Which is Seen, and That Which is Not Seen
(1850)

In economics, an act, a habit, an institution, or a law gives birth not only to one effect, but also to a whole series of effects. Of these effects, the first only is seen immediately; it manifests itself simultaneously with its cause; it is seen. The others unfold in succession and they are not seen. But it would be well for us if they were foreseen.

Between a good and a bad economist this constitutes the whole difference: the one takes account of the visible effect; the other takes account both of the effects which are seen, and also of those which it is necessary to foresee.

I. The Broken Window

Have you ever witnessed the anger of the good shopkeeper when his careless son happened to break a square of glass? If you have been present at such a scene, you will bear witness to the fact, that one of the spectators would offer the unfortunate owner this consolation, "Everybody must live, and what would become of the glaziers if panes of glass were never broken?"

Now, this form of condolence contains an entire theory, which it will be well to show up in this simple case, seeing that it is precisely the same as that which, unhappily, regulates the greater part of our economical institutions.

Suppose it cost six francs to repair the damage, and you say that the accident brings six francs to the glazier's trade—that it encourages that trade to the amount of six francs—I grant it; you reason justly. The glazier comes, performs his task, receives his six francs, rubs his hands, and, in his heart, blesses the careless child. All this is that which is seen.

But if you come to the conclusion that it is a good thing to break windows, that it causes money to circulate, and that the encouragement of industry in general will result, you will oblige me to call out, "Stop there! Your theory is confined to that which is seen; it takes no account of that which is not seen."

> It is not seen that as our shopkeeper has spent six francs upon one thing, he cannot spend them upon another. It is not seen that if he had not had a window to replace, he would, perhaps, have replaced his old shoes, or added another book to his library. In short, he would have employed his six francs in some way.

Let us take a view of industry in general. The window being broken, the glazier's trade is encouraged to the amount of six francs; this is that which is seen. If the window had not been broken, the shoemaker's trade (or some other) would have been encouraged to the amount of six francs; this is that which is not seen.

And if that which is not seen is taken into consideration, it will be understood that neither industry in general, nor the sum total of national labour, is affected, whether windows are broken or not.

"Society loses the value of things which are uselessly destroyed;" and we must assent to a maxim which will make the hair of protectionists stand on end—To break, to spoil, to waste, is not to encourage national labour; or, more briefly, "destruction is not profit."

The reader must take care to remember that there are not two persons only, but three concerned in the little scene which I have submitted to his attention.

> One of them represents the consumer, reduced, by an act of destruction, to one enjoyment instead of two.

> Another under the title of the glazier, shows us the producer, whose trade is encouraged by the accident.

> The third is the shoemaker (or some other tradesman), whose labour suffers proportionately by the same cause.

It is this third person who is always kept in the shade, and who, personating that which is not seen, is a necessary element of the problem. It is he who shows us how absurd it is to think we see a profit in an act of destruction.

Therefore, if you will only go to the root of all the arguments which are adduced in its favour, all you will find will be the paraphrase of this vulgar saying, "What would become of the glaziers, if nobody ever broke windows?"

François-René de Chateaubriand (1768-1848), from *Memoirs from Beyond the Grave*

There are two consequences in history; an immediate one, which is instantly recognized, and one in the distance, which is not at first perceived.

These consequences often contradict each other; the former are the results of our own limited wisdom, the latter, those of that wisdom which endures.

The providential event appears after the human event. God rises up behind men. Deny, if you will, the supreme counsel; disown its action; dispute about words; designate, by the term, force of circumstances, or reason, what the vulgar call Providence; but look to the end of an accomplished fact, and you will see that it has always produced the contrary of what was expected from it, if it was not established at first upon morality and justice.

Adam Smith (1723-1790), from *An Inquiry into the Nature and Causes of the Wealth of Nations* (1776)

As every individual, therefore, endeavors as much as he can both to employ his capital in the support of domestic industry, and so to direct that industry that its produce may be of the greatest value; every individual necessarily labors to render the annual revenue of the society as great as he can.

He generally, indeed, neither intends to promote the public interest, nor knows how much he is promoting it. By preferring the support of domestic to that of foreign industry, he intends only his own security; and by directing that industry in such a manner as its produce may be of the greatest value, he intends only his own gain, and he is in this, as in many other cases, led by an invisible hand to promote an end which was no part of his intention.

Nor is it always the worse for the society that it was no part of it. By pursuing his own interest, he frequently promotes that of the society more effectually than when he really intends to promote it. I have never known much good done by those who affected to trade for the public good. It is an affectation, indeed, not very common among merchants, and very few words need be employed in dissuading them from it.

THE SCHOOL OF
PYTHAGORAS™

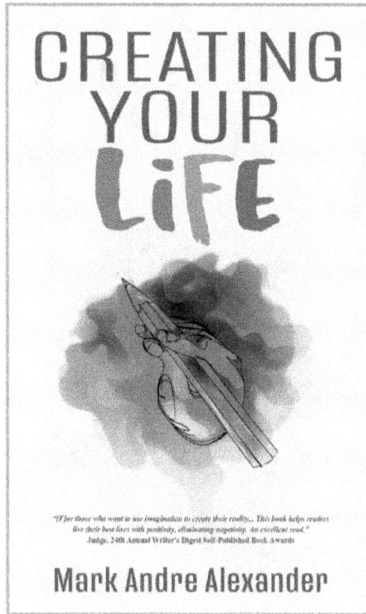

"This book is a truly powerful and important work for young and old alike. This is required reading for my two children. Mark Alexander takes a no nonsense, practical approach to empowering, equipping, and informing people to live their best lives." — Rashiid K. Coleman

"This book is helping me see that I was beating myself up. I was creating and holding on to the picture that if I was stressed I should get migraines. I was creating my own migraines. So I worked with a friend and we changed the picture. Every day I let go of the old picture and adopt the new picture of being a person free from migraines. And it's working!" — Rose Mulvey

"This is an EXCELLENT book! I love it and strongly recommend it." — Glenn E. Meder

SEX and ROMANCE

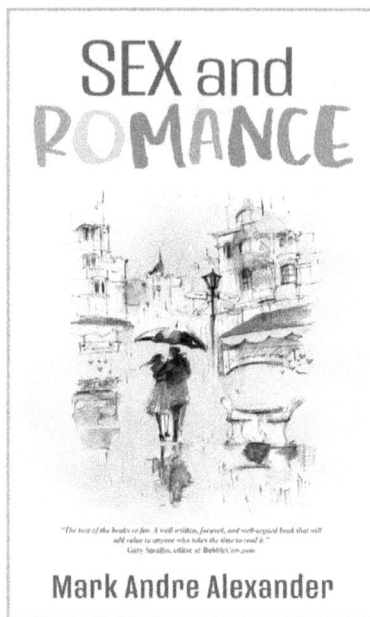

"The best of the books so far. A well-written, focused, and well-argued book that will add value to anyone who takes the time to read it."
Gary Smailes, editor at BubbleCow.com

Mark Andre Alexander

"The best of the books so far. A well-written, focused, and well-argued book that will add value to anyone who takes the time to read it." — Gary Smailes, editor at BubbleCow.com.

"I was blown away. Although it's a fairly short read, Mr. Alexander has packed a huge amount of valuable and perceptive information for readers...Parents, teachers, counselors, clergymen, and basically anyone working and counseling teens and tweens will find this book an invaluable resource...filled with insightful quotes, common sense advice, and delightful prose." — Susan Barton - eBook Review Gal

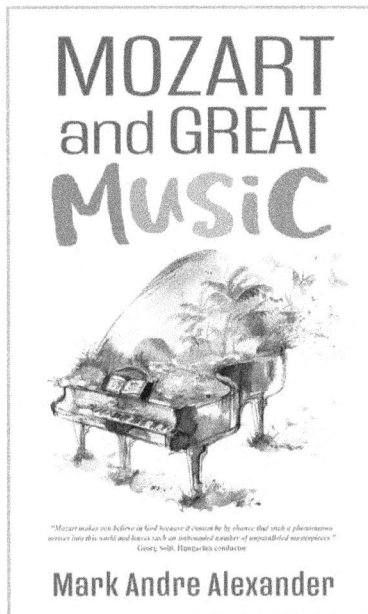

> "Mozart's joy is made of serenity, and a phrase of his music is like a calm thought; his simplicity is merely purity. It is a crystalline thing in which all the emotions play a role, but as if already celestially transposed." — André Gide, Nobel Prize-winning author

> "Mozart makes you believe in God because it cannot be by chance that such a phenomenon arrives into this world and leaves such an unbounded number of unparalleled masterpieces." — Georg Solti, conductor

> "It is thanks to Mozart that I have devoted my life to music...Mozart is the highest, the culminating point that beauty has attained in the sphere of music. Mozart is the musical Christ." — Piotr Tchaikovsky, Russian composer

About the Author

Mark Andre Alexander has a B.A. in English and an M.A. in Organization and Management Development. He works in Silicon Valley helping people take their next step. He's a happy soul, a composer and musician, and likes to make people laugh.

Occasionally he publishes articles and books. He's married to a woman who improves him just by being present, and he believes everyone is on a journey to learn how to give and receive divine love.

Books in the series *A Lifetime of Learning*
Creating Your Life (A Lifetime of Learning, Book 1)
Money and Wealth (A Lifetime of Learning, Book 2)
Sex and Romance (A Lifetime of Learning, Book 3)
Mozart and Great Music (A Lifetime of Learning, Book 4)

Forthcoming topics in the series include Shakespeare, great literature, the ancient Greeks, language, rhetoric, law, liberty, virtue, vice, education, training, science, truth, soul, and spirit.

Other books
Handbook for Advanced Souls: Eternal Reminders for the Present Moment

Public domain works edited by Mark Andre Alexander
Shakespeare's Law and Latin by Sir George Greenwood, M.P.
The George Greenwood Collection
Hamlet and the Scottish Succession by Lilian Winstanley

THE SCHOOL OF
PYTHAGORAS™

www.ingramcontent.com/pod-product-compliance
Lightning Source LLC
Chambersburg PA
CBHW070930210326
41520CB00021B/6873